Casa Pueblo

A PUERTO RICAN MODEL
OF SELF-GOVERNANCE

Alexis Massol González

Translated by

Ashwin Ravikumar and
Paul A. Schroeder Rodríguez

LEVER
PRESS

DOI: https://doi.org/10.3998/mpub.12467264
Print ISBN: 978-1-64315-034-5
Open access ISBN: 978-1-64315-029-1

Published in the United States of America by Lever Press, in partnership with
Amherst College Press and Michigan Publishing

Contents

Member Institution Acknowledgments

Lever Press is a joint venture. This work was made possible by the generous support of Lever Press member libraries from the following institutions:

Adrian College

Agnes Scott College

Allegheny College

Amherst College

Bard College

Berea College

Bowdoin College

Carleton College

Claremont Graduate
   University

Claremont McKenna College

Clark Atlanta University

Coe College

College of Saint Benedict /
   Saint John's University

The College of Wooster

Denison University

DePauw University

Earlham College

Furman University

Grinnell College

Hamilton College

Harvey Mudd College

Haverford College

Hollins University

Keck Graduate Institute

Kenyon College

Knox College

Lafayette College Library

Lake Forest College

Macalester College

Middlebury College

Morehouse College
Oberlin College
Pitzer College
Pomona College
Rollins College
Santa Clara University
Scripps College
Sewanee: The University of the South
Skidmore College
Smith College
Spelman College
St. Lawrence University
St. Olaf College
Susquehanna University
Swarthmore College
Trinity University
Union College
University of Puget Sound
Ursinus College
Vassar College
Washington and Lee University
Whitman College
Willamette University
Williams College

Bordonua
A large, deep-body bass guitar often with three sound holes; it is the third and lowest stringed instrument in the orquesta típica puertorriqueña.

Boricua
The Puerto Rican people, the inhabitants and citizens of the Puerto Rico and their descendants, both on the island and in the diaspora.

Borinquen
The precolonial name of the island nation of Puerto Rico in the language of the Indigenous Taíno people.

Borinqueño
A resident of Borinquen.

Cuatro
A ten-stringed musical instrument in the guitar family that is shaped more like a viola; it is the middle voice in the orquesta típica puertorriqueña.

Décima

In Hispanic culture, a poetic form of ten lines, usually performed as a song consisting of forty-four lines with a four-line introductory stanza. In Puerto Rico, décimas are accompanied by the orquesta típica and singers often challenge each other to improvise verses in the rhyming scheme ABBAACCDDC.

Don, Doña

Literally "Mister" or "Missus," these terms are used as expressions of respect, courtesy, social distinction, or when a person is considered very intelligent or accomplished.

Jíbaro

Refers to the countryside people in the mountains of Puerto Rico who farm the land in a traditional way. The jíbaro is a self-subsistence farmer, and an iconic reflection of the indefatigable spirit of the Puerto Rican people.

Maestro

Teacher or master, often used as a term of respect for wise or learned people.

Mapeyé

A musical term, it refers to "seis mapeyé," a harmonic style of jíbaro dance music that is closely associated with the décima lyric/poetic form. The well-known Puerto Rican music group Mapeyé takes its name from this form.

Orquesta típica

Sometimes simply called "típica" is a term that varies from country to country in Latin America. In Puerto Rico a típica is a jíbaro musical group that usually features a cuatro, tiple, bordonua, possible guitar, and percussion instruments like a güiro (a dried gourd with scores on it that is scraped rhythmically with a kind of metal comb) and/or bongo drums. The sound of the orquesta típica is a source of Puerto Rican national pride and cultural unity.

Pasteles
A cherished culinary treat in Puerto Rico, especially around Christmastime. The masa (dough) is made of green banana, green plantain, white yautía, potato, and tropical pumpkins known as calabazas. It is seasoned with liquid from a meat mixture, milk, and annatto oil, and is a cousin to the Mexican tamale. Fillings can range from vegetables, poultry, fish, pork, and game.

Pueblo
A town where commerce and natural resources are produced and marketed; also, the group of those people who live in a town, region, or country and derive their group cultural identity from that place.

Tiple
A twelve-stringed instrument in the guitar family, used extensively in Puerto Rican traditional music; the highest-pitched instrument in the orquest típica.

Introduction

Casa Pueblo (casapueblo.org) is a community-based organization in Adjuntas, a municipality of approximately 20,000 people in the lush subtropical mountains of south-central Puerto Rico. The group started as a loose gathering of people joined in opposition to a series of planned open-pit mines in the 1970s. It quickly grew in number and organizational acuity to the point that by 1995, the group had put a definite stop to all mining in the region. A major watershed had been saved, and a major environmental catastrophe had been averted. But Casa Pueblo did not stop there. Instead, the group moved swiftly from protesting mines to proposing and implementing far-reaching solutions to further benefit the natural environment and the people who live in it. Casa Pueblo calls itself a sustainable project of community self-governance, a radical bottom-up alternative for transforming the social and political colonial model in Puerto Rico.

With a small and dedicated staff, Casa Pueblo today administers a Forest School of approximately 150 acres, an income-generating coffee plantation that produces 100% arabica seeds for their signature *Madre Isla Coffee*, an ecological guesthouse, a solar-powered radio station, a solar-powered movie theater, and a growing solar grid that functions as a cooperative. Its base of operations is a welcoming 1920s-era house in the center of Adjuntas that doubles as a community center and community refuge, as in the aftermath of Hurricane Maria, when hundreds plugged into solar-powered outlets there to run medical equipment, while thousands more benefited from information broadcast on the solar-powered radio station. Naomi Klein wrote a compelling and widely circulated piece on these and other initiatives post-Maria, for *The Intercept*.

More broadly, the Casa Pueblo house is the physical manifestation of what can happen when seeds of hope are carefully planted and cultivated in a sustained and thoughtful fashion. The fruits are impressive: not a top-down utopia imagined for some time in the far-off future, but a living, breathing, bottom-up, and ever-evolving sustainable community on our planet today. Casa Pueblo's most recent campaign to liberate Puerto Rico from fossil fuels by way of solar power is an example. Since Hurricane Maria in 2017, Casa Pueblo has expanded its solar power grid beyond its own properties and is now on track to making Adjuntas the first fully solar-powered municipality in Puerto Rico, and perhaps the world, even as it spearheads local efforts to confront the Covid-19 pandemic. In these and other ways, Casa Pueblo leads by example, demonstrating how community self-governance and community-based mutual aid can deliver health, safety, and sustainability when the government does not.

Alexis Massol González, a co-founder of Casa Pueblo and the recipient of the 2002 Goldman Prize (popularly known as the Environmental Nobel Prize), reflects in this book on the extraordinary 40-year history of Casa Pueblo and how the principle of *community self-governance* (*autogestión comunitaria*) emerged over time as a bottom-up approach to community organizing, in contrast to approaches that rely on governments and distant non-profits. In a soon-to-be-published study of Casa Pueblo and two similar grassroots organizations—the Zapatista Army of National Liberation in Mexico and the Boggs Center in Detroit—philosopher Gregory Fernando Pappas notes that the three groups "practice horizontal models of 'conviviality'. They share a communitarian, holistic, ecological, and experimental approach to ameliorating injustices. They have experimented with community-based transformative justice in all spheres of life. They have proclaimed openly that the preferred way to move forward to address injustices is via a radical conception of democracy . . . from the ground up."[1] Massol González puts it as follows: "Since its foundation in 1980, Casa Pueblo has set in motion an alternative process, a radical response to the barriers imposed by Puerto Rico's colonial model of representative democracy. Community self-governance embraces different sectors and actors without falling into the naive optimism of those who would simply change bad rulers and politicians, or the passive pessimism of those who oppose alternatives at every turn."[2]

Our greatest hope is that these profound lessons in community self-governance and sustainable conviviality will move many to support the work of Casa Pueblo, and inspire many more to adapt these valuable lessons to their own communities and contexts.

ABOUT THIS TRANSLATION

In January of 2020, Ashwin J. Ravikumar and Paul A. Schroeder Rodríguez took a group of twelve Amherst College students to Puerto Rico as part of a course, *Climate Change and Social Justice in Puerto Rico.* We are professors from different academic backgrounds: Paul is a scholar of Latin American cinema in the Spanish Department, and Ashwin is a political ecologist in the Department of Environmental Studies who works with Indigenous communities in the Peruvian Amazon. We collaborated to stage this interdisciplinary course out of a shared understanding that culture is central to social and political movements and that in Puerto Rico, an island nation, social and political movements are on the front lines of the climate crisis. With generous financial support from the Amherst College Dean of Faculty, guidance from our Center for Community Engagement, and logistical support from Spanish

Studies Abroad (an Amherst-based provider of study abroad programs in Spain and Latin America), we designed an innovative place-based learning experience aligned with the broad goals of a liberal arts education in the areas of writing, critical thinking, and community engagement.

Because the trip took place before the semester officially began and therefore before students had a chance to get to know one another, we conducted a one-day, pre-departure orientation filled with social icebreakers and logistical information. Amherst College's Center for Teaching and Learning provided instrumental pedagogical support in designing this orientation workshop. The trip provided more opportunities for the students to learn from each other and from several grassroots organizations that work on alternative models of climate justice, community-based land management, and art for social justice. Our base of operations in San Juan was the University of Sagrado Corazón, an urban oasis of green in the populous Santurce neighborhood of San Juan. Except for two overnight trips, one to Vieques and the other to the town of Adjuntas, each day was designed as a day trip. A student favorite was the visit to Corredor Yaguazo, a community-based land management organization founded in the 1980s by local resident Pedro Carrión. A low-income resident of the area himself, he formed the organization to resist the displacement of the community from the mangrove forest lands that nearby chemical plants wanted to acquire. Corredor Yaguazo now teaches young people how to protect and restore the coastal mangroves of the Ciénaga las Cu-cha-ri-llas Natural Reserve, which plays a crucial role in protecting Puerto Rico from hurricane storm surges. Students learned about the origins of this community-based organization from its founder and planted mangrove saplings.

In San Juan, staff from the Museum of Contemporary Art in Santurce took us on a walking tour of the neighboring community, Alto del Cabro where residents worked with artists to create murals celebrating the community's connection to its immediate urban environment and the adjacent Condado lagoon. Also in San Juan, the G-8, Inc. (Group of The Eight Communities Surrounding the Caño) gave us a tour of Caño Martín Peña, a polluted tidal channel that the organization is working to rehabilitate. G-8, Inc. manages a community land trust, the first of its kind in Puerto Rico, designed to guard against real estate speculators and developers keen to expand San Juan's financial district into the G-8 area.

All the organizations we visited—including two in Vieques, the Fortín Conde de Mirasol Cultural Center, and the Vieques National Wildlife Refuge—have been busy rebuilding after Hurricane Maria, which devastated the Puerto Rican archipelago in 2017. All are focusing on long-term social and ecological resilience. Among such groups, Casa Pueblo stands out because of its long history and list of accomplishments.

The timing of our visit was fortuitous. Just a month before we visited, the book you are reading had been published in Spanish. We humbly asked Alexis Massol González, the book's author and a leader of Casa Pueblo, what he thought of the idea of students in the class taking on the translation as a collaborative project. To our surprise, he kindly asked that we follow up with him via email. Soon after our return to Amherst, we conducted a translation mini-workshop with excerpts from the original text. The exercise confirmed both the high quality of students' translations and their enthusiasm for the project. So, with a sample translation signaling our seriousness of purpose, we reached out to Alexis Massol González, who in turn consulted with the rest of the members of Casa Pueblo. The group enthusiastically accepted the proposal.

Alongside this translation project, students were hard at work developing solidarity projects. When the Covid-19 pandemic struck Massachusetts in March 2020, they were deep in the planning stages of bringing community leaders and artists from Puerto Rico to Western Massachusetts for an event with Holyoke High School, a nearby school with a majority Puerto Rican student body.

Unable to organize in-person events to build solidarity and community between Amherst College students, Holyoke High School students, and Puerto Rican community leaders, we decided to devote the rest of the class to this translation.

As a first step, students worked in pairs to translate approximately two chapters each. The translation teams then exchanged their work to offer feedback and address any inconsistencies between versions. During class time, we discussed concepts and phrases that presented challenges, both in specific parts of the text and in its guiding ideas, generating a glossary of commonly used terms in the process. The students then began the second round of translations, which they turned in at the end of the semester. During summer 2020, we (Ashwin and Paul) edited and polished the students' second round of translations and translated a new final chapter that Mr. Massol González wrote about the impact of Covid-19 on Casa Pueblo's many initiatives. Finally, we shared the translation with Casa Pueblo and incorporated their feedback into the final text. In this way, our translation project combines Casa Pueblo's vision of working towards the common good with the kind of collaborative praxis and emphasis on education that has defined their approach to solving problems.

We feel honored and proud to share this collaborative translation with English-language readers everywhere; and privileged to have done so in collaboration with Beth Bouloukos, Amanda Karby, Dorothy P. Snyder, and the rest of the team at Lever Press, a global leader in born-digital, peer reviewed, open access monograph publishing.

Ashwin J. Ravikumar and Paul A. Schroeder Rodríguez

Student translators:
Abner Aldarondo
Tanya A. Calvin
Lucheyla Celestino

Alexis Chávez Salinas
Corina E. Cobb
Hubert E. Ford
Molly Malczynski
Joseph A. Ramesar
Kyabeth Rincón
Jeffrey Suliveres
Augusta S. Weiss
Javier F. Whitaker Castañeda

PART I

CHRONICLES OF AN ANTI-MINING CAMPAIGN

CHAPTER 1

HOW AN ANTI-MINING STRUGGLE GAVE SHAPE TO OUR COMMUNITY

Panoramic view of the town of Adjuntas, in the central mountains of Puerto Rico. January 29, 2020.

A word without action is empty, an action without words is blind, and both actions and words are dead without the spirit of the community.

—NASA Project, Toribio, Cauca, Colombia

THE CONCEPT OF COMMUNITY

The term *community* is one of the most used in the social sciences. It refers to a particular relationship between a social group and a territory. Community is a word that evokes multiple ideas. It can be defined as a group of people that live in a defined geographic space and share common interests, traditions, customs, history, and identity. Communities create a sense of belonging by sharing experiences of everyday life, conflicts and struggles, and by seeking to satisfy their needs and resolve their problems together. José Luis Saballos Velásquez, in his 2016 doctoral thesis at the University of the Basque Country, defines life in community as "a collective act of solidarity, cooperation, and fraternity between people, propagated through the continuous cultivation of attitudes and behaviors including empathy, reciprocity, trust, and warmth. Community is, then, an important space for the flourishing of the most noble human values and the common good." We can also reference the definition proposed by the social psychologist Dr. Maritza Montero: "a community is a social group that is constantly transforming and evolving; it creates feelings of belonging and identity through interpersonal relations and reinforces its members' awareness of themselves as a group in unity and social potential."

COMMUNITY: THE STARTING POINT FOR OUR WORK

Casa Pueblo began as an arts and culture initiative to stop a mining proposal in the municipalities of Adjuntas, Utuado, Lares, Jayuya, and Ponce. We held our first Arts and Culture Workshop in 1980 in Adjuntas, and in so doing, joined a far-reaching environmental movement that had been growing since the 1960s and that provided a basis for our defense of non-renewable natural resources. In essence, the Arts and Culture Workshop connected the fight against mining with a larger national strategy, using local community organizing as a starting point. With the support, solidarity, and fighting spirit of a wide range of groups like Misión Industrial,

Movimiento Pro Independencia, Partido Independentista Puer-torriqueño, Vanguardia Popular, and the Liga Socialista Puer-torriqueña, among others, we successfully stopped mining from ruining our environment and our livelihoods. In the process, we planted the seeds for what people began to call Casa Pueblo, after the old house in the town center where we set up headquarters in 1985.

Three major events led to the creation of the Workshop. The first was a successful struggle to remove asbestos in all public schools in Adjuntas. Two of the founders of the Workshop began their work as community leaders in this struggle: Tinti Deyá and Noemilda Vélez, the president and vice president, respectively, of the local teachers' federation. The second was the formation of a local committee to support the removal of the U.S. Navy from Vieques. Two young people from Adjuntas, Lourdes Torres and María Jiménez, joined the Workshop through this struggle. Third, we had friends in Adjuntas who were genuinely interested in com-ing together to address the needs of our community, including leaders like Josie Ballester who represented key local constituen-cies. Then, on August 31, 1980, a national issue was added to the first two: the headlines of the newspaper *El Mundo* announced that the government had approved plans for U.S. mining compa-nies to start exploiting an estimated $5 billion in copper, gold, and silver resources in Puerto Rico. At first, it seemed that the decision was final, that it would be impossible to overturn. After all, the government had already approved open-pit mining at seventeen sites in Adjuntas, Utuado, Lares, Jayuya, and Ponce; the Planning Board marked 37,000 acres of land for this purpose; and the mul-tinational companies AMAX and Kennecott owned the land in and around the two main deposits, in Calá Abajo and Piedra Hueca, along with land purchases for a refinery and a foundry by the coast in Guayanilla.

The original core group of anti-mining activists included stu-dents, teachers, workers, and two engineers. The group's diverse expertise and educational backgrounds helped us to analyze the mining proposal from both a scientific and a political perspective, and to develop an appropriate strategy to better confront it. The group identified the underlying issue as environmental colonialism, whereby a few capitalist companies from the United States take over and profit from our raw materials, leaving us with nothing but environmental destruction. Can you imagine your landscape reduced into a giant mound of rubble, with no mountains, birds, flowers, or rivers? Choosing the group's name generated an intense debate. The choice was not easy. Some preferred to call it the *Anti-mining Committee*. Others wanted a name that centered our anti-imperialist stance. Still others wanted a name that would be more inclusive to wide sectors of the local community. After several meetings, the organization was named *The Arts and Culture Workshop of Adjuntas*. Our areas of focus from the start were to address people's necessities, advocate for human rights, fight displacement, preserve the integrity of our water and land, and to articulate an alternative development model based on community self-governance.

A PATRIOT JOINS THE CAUSE

For our first public activity as a Workshop, on April 19, 1981, we decided to recover what we called the Sun of Adjuntas, an Indigenous monolith marked with petroglyphs, and place it in the public plaza as a historic monument to our Taíno heritage. Indigenous dancers from Jayuya participated in the event, a group of local youths unveiled the monument, and there was live music. About 300 people attended, and the event was a resounding success. Before the activities, we had an enriching experience with the poet and Puerto Rican nationalist and patriot, Juan Antonio Corretjer, a well-known poet and opponent of U.S. imperialism in Puerto Rico. Before the Workshop was formed, the Puerto Rican Socialist League, which Corretjer helped lead, had its own anti-mining chapter in Adjuntas. In fact, some members of the League joined our group; don Juan and doña Consuela, his wife and fellow leader in the League, frequented our town. They were not strangers to the residents of Adjuntas, nor to the local police. Soon, the two would become key members of our organization.

For the unveiling of the monolith, don Juan had been invited as a speaker, along with Luis F. Camacho, then-president of the Bar Association, and Dr. Ricardo Alegría, founder of the Institute of Puerto Rican Culture. Unfortunately, a few days before the event, Alegría and Camacho had to cancel, leaving only the poet to speak at the event. Having just one voice at an event involving so many individuals and groups presented a problem of balance. After several sometimes bitter internal discussions, we met with don Juan in person. Having patiently heard the arguments of those who believed he should speak and those who believed he should not, Corretjer finally said: "As part of an orchestra, the sound of my words would be very good; but as a soloist, the same sound would be quite bad."

This was an important learning experience for us, as it reinforced our own vision of collective action. From then on, Corretjer's wisdom always accompanied us. That lesson, that we are an orchestra, stronger with our multitude of voices, stays with us today. When outside actors try to usurp the community spaces that we have claimed through hard and under-appreciated work, we remember that we represent a collective of voices, and that our community belongs to all of us. Afterwards, in his humble home, the poet and patriot told us that mining doesn't just generate private profits for U.S. firms without benefiting Puerto Rican workers. The main issue, he argued, was the physical destruction of our national territory and its conversion into a place that is not suitable for collective living. It was a moral and ethical issue of tremendous scale, so much so that the very survival of Puerto Rico as a nation was at stake.

Five months later, we were preparing to hold our first anti-mining rally. We started to work with tremendous confidence and a somewhat distorted view of the town's level of consciousness about the issue. The first step was to educate ourselves about what mining in our community would entail, and what consequences it would have for the environment and for people. We organized various conferences with scientists and technicians who knew about the topic, like Dr. Tomás Morales Cardona, who brought us technical materials and a very important flyer with the headline *Environmental Colonialism*. Dr. Neftalí García and others who participated in the conference were our first teachers in this process. We had differences with some of them, as is natural. On one hand, they exposed the gravity of the environmental dangers posed by mining. On the other hand, they left the door open to the possibility that mining could be useful to Puerto Rico, whether it became an independent republic or remained a colony, if it was done within certain restrictions.

This created much confusion in the Workshop and in the public at large. We reminded some participants from the neighborhood of Tanamá to feel free to interrupt the speakers to ask if they were for or against the mining. In one talk in the Pellejas neighborhood, two courageous jíbaros, Juan Rivera and Pablo Natal, offered that "Puerto Rico cannot handle mines," echoing Corretjer. Given the conflicting messages from experts, we decided to educate ourselves. We subscribed to a British scientific magazine about mining. This gave us access to very important technical information about global mining, the fluctuations in the value of minerals, and what mining companies like AMAX and Kennecott were planning to do; all information that was not widely known in Puerto Rico. We also gained access to a bulletin edited by the United States Bureau of Mines. A North American group of ecologists gave us access to a video about environmental destruction in the mines of the Appalachian Mountains, and a Workshop facilitator provided another video about copper mines in Chile. We purchased the public performance rights to an episode of the popular Tommy Muñiz TV Show in which he presented a magnificent documentary about copper mines in Utah, to use in our education efforts. With the help of some colleagues, we obtained the official documents for previous mining proposals and permits, as well as those being promoted by AMAX and Kennecott at the time. For several months, we studied all this information.

Slowly but surely, we began to form our own political interpretation and our own scientific analysis of mining. Technical terms became part of our regular vocabulary as we learned about porphyry copper, sulfuric material, open-pit mining, chalcopyrites, mine tailings, foundries, and refineries. We learned that the mining proposal called for open-pit mines, enormous craters that could reach a mile in diameter and 2,000 feet in depth, at every one of the seventeen deposits discovered in Puerto Rico. We learned that open mining was the only feasible technique to extract the copper ore mineral, known as porphyry, and that copper, gold, silver, and the other minerals associated with them are dispersed in various places and at different depths, hence the need for open-pit mining. We learned all of this little by little, turning science into an educational instrument and a tool of the struggle. At the end of this learning process, we concluded that open-pit mining was not compatible with our environment, and that it would destroy the fabric of our community. The forests, watersheds, rivers, and people of Puerto Rico, a small island, simply could not withstand mining. Through this educational process we also learned that our campaign aligned with the position of patriots like Corretjer and the wisdom of the jíbaros, the country folk who have farmed and stewarded the lands and waters of Puerto Rico for generations. We adopted the motto *Republic or Colony, Zero Mines in Puerto Rico*. In other words, whether Puerto Rico remains a colony of the United States or becomes an independent Republic, we would oppose mining. This position became a key element of our own voice.

THE CONCEPT OF "ONE'S OWN VOICE"

The position of the Workshop as summarized in our new motto was supported by the community, but it went against the opinion of practically every major power broker across the Puerto Rican political spectrum. Some pushed for mining along with the continued colonial status of Puerto Rico; others supported mining in the context of Puerto Rican statehood; still others were pro-independence and pro-mining. The takeaway for us was that we needed to learn as much as we could about mining to communicate our position to people with different views on Puerto Rico's colonial status. Too often, the voice of the community–one's own voice–is lost when the struggle is handed over to political parties and politicians, no matter how good their intentions. It's one thing when they are in the opposition, and quite another when they are in power. By rigorously educating ourselves and having a clear message, we have been able to stay true to our own voice, to create our own identity, to write our organization's own history, lift our self-esteem, and participate enthusiastically in advancing the goals of the community. All of this also helps to break submissive styles of community participation forged under foreign domination and to help people unite in struggle as equals. During this process, foreign domination began to loosen, along with our own colonized ways of relating that pit us against each other. At its core, the locally organized community is a starting point for developing one's own voice. Having one's own voice as a self-governing community organization allows us to set our own rules as we struggle and work towards reaching our goals. That voice represents a range of values, positions, and our own norms regulating the group's conduct. It clarifies our group's strategy. It provides us with a clear and unambiguous message that guides our freely decided course of action. It breaks dependencies. The concept of one's own voice avoids confusion among the people and protects community organizations from those who would use their work to advance their own political agendas and personal prestige.

THE PRINCIPLES OF IDENTITY, OPPOSITION, AND TOTALITY

A self-governing community organization that acts in accordance with its own voice enters a natural process of weaving its own *identity*. Identity is everything that characterizes and distinguishes an individual from others. It distinguishes a person from a group, and a group from another group. It embraces what a person or group does, how they do it, the working styles and beliefs that they deploy, and the history that they write. On the other hand, the principle of *opposition* refers to clearly identifying the true adversary. It does not confuse those who favor mining in the belief that it would be good for the community with those who push the project forward only for private gain, like the government, politicians, political parties, and mining companies. The struggle is an affirmation of one's own voice and identity, but it has many adversaries. By clarifying who the adversary is, we can avoid making mistakes when establishing alliances. The principle of *totality* refers to having a view, not of particular facts, but of the whole situation, including the history and the context of that situation. The mining project was not an isolated issue, it was part of an integral economic development scheme for the whole country called the Plan 2020, which I will be discussing later in the book. The combination of these three principles—identity, opposition, and totality—reinforces good governance, avoids errors, and clarifies doubts. The three go hand in hand; ignoring this fact weakens our capacity for effective action. These three principles have central importance for the sociologist Alain Touraine, who asks: "If one is to fight, should one not know in whose name one is fighting against, and on what grounds?"

CHAPTER 2

FIRST ANTI-MINING JOURNEY

The first anti-mining campaign took place with an audience of one. September 4, 1981.

YES TO LIFE, NO TO MINING

In 1981, we launched a neighborhood-by-neighborhood campaign to continue the anti-mining struggle under the slogan *Yes to Life, No to Mining*. It was an invitation to our neighbors to join us in joyful struggle. The objective was to inform people about the negative impact of mining, and to begin building a broad coalition of communities to stop the destruction of 37,000 acres where thousands of Puerto Rican families had built their homes and communities. This was another important argument in our campaign: beyond the physical destruction of mining, we were also at risk of being displaced by companies from the United States. During this phase of the campaign, a team would go house to house in each neighborhood, sharing information and extending an invitation to discuss the issue further. Then, on a night and place chosen by the neighbors, we would start the community forum with an explanation of the mining issue, using understandable vocabulary and slides that illustrated the likely impacts of the mines. We focused our conversations on the impact that the mining activity would have on each neighborhood. Attendance never fell below 80 participants.

We put a lot of effort and patience into this preparatory work and carried out the information sessions in the Pellejas, Vegas Arriba, Vegas Abajo, Juan González, Tanamá, and Vacas Saltillo neighborhoods. We also visited the Adjuntas high school and put on a larger event in the town's central plaza. We always found ourselves in the company of some people who were in favor of the mining project. In their view, mining seemed to be a better option than the economic neglect and lack of opportunity that they were facing. Regardless, we carried on with our efforts not just to educate, but also to strengthen the local community organization. It was during this time that we held our first press conference, at The Bar Association of Puerto Rico in San Juan. In attendance were reporters from TV Channels 2, 4, and Telemundo; the Associated Press; WKAQ Radio; and the newspapers *Claridad, El Reportero, El*

Mundo, and *El Nuevo Día*. This was a new experience for our group. Telemundo did a feature from Adjuntas with Jorge Rivera Nieves, in which members of the Arts and Culture Workshop explained our struggles at the local and national levels. The press conference strengthened our learning and communications skills, allowed us to make mistakes, and helped us develop our ability to speak with our own voice.

We held our first anti-mining workshop from September 4 to 6, 1981 in Adjuntas. On the first day, only one person attended; he stood near the stage. Despite our audience of one, there were many police officers surrounding us in the public plaza. We were joined on stage by Juan Antonio Corretjer, Consuelo Lee, and Carmín Pérez. Tony Rivera and the Grupo Mapeyé oversaw the cultural activities. Singers included Amado Vélez, Aníbal Soto, and Ismael Vélez, along with the family and friends of Noemilda Vélez, the workshop leader. Brunilda García and Iris Martínez donated their art, while the sons and daughters of our friends Noé and Tinti took care of other tasks. I remember that on one of the days, the invited speaker was an archeologist who spoke about digs in the mining zone and how they would be affected. He started to "spit revolutionary fire," talking about socialism, the Cuban Revolution, armed struggle, and Puerto Rican independence as the only way for the town to avoid impending destruction. We asked him to concentrate on the assigned topic, but when he continued his diatribe, we had to take more extreme intervention measures and lowered the volume of the sound system until he stopped.

The town's participation in the First Anti-Mining Workshop was very low. We were disappointed with the turnout, especially since we had put so much effort into organizing the event. Moreover, the situation provoked a profound debate that ended with more than half of the leaders leaving the group. There were many different arguments presented. Some suggested that our status as a colony translated into impotence, low self-esteem, and dependence on federal "help." Others derided telenovelas (the soap operas on Spanish language television), dancing, drinking, and betting as forms of entertainment that generated alienation. Some even argued that stopping the mines would require organizing at the level of political parties, not at the community level. On the other hand, we realized that it was one thing to visit a community and ask people to listen, and quite another for that community to support our struggle and participate in it. We understood that the correct approach was not what our archeologist friend attempted, nor was it correct to merely yell chants. We knew for a fact that many people were very afraid of getting involved in our struggle, given the government's strong threats of repression and harassment. The stigma of communism, subversive activity, and pro-independence nationalism weighed heavily on the people. We asked ourselves, how can we get the community more involved without sacrificing our core principles?

Winning the hearts of townspeople so that they might defend their own community and territory became an urgent goal, but it was very hard to get people to feel empowered to act on issues that affected everyone. The Arts and Culture Workshop would soon take up the challenge of developing better methods to achieve this fundamental objective; meanwhile we kept applying ourselves. Throughout 1981, we saw proof of the group's ability and determination to work hard. That year the group participated in historic events, including conferences on the abolition of slavery in Puerto Rico; educational events about the life and work of one of founders of the Puerto Rican independence movement, Ramón Emeterio Betances; screenings of important films like *Taíno Heritage* and *Isla de Mona* in schools and neighborhoods; and kite-making workshops. On November 19, 20, and 21 of that year, we held events examining Christopher Columbus's arrival in Puerto Rico, alongside the opening of our bookstore, Librería Palenque. Professor Calixta Vélez held a workshop on children's games in the public plaza, and Elizam Escobar, an activist for independence and former prisoner of war, exhibited his paintings. The poet don Juan Antonio Corretjer gave a lecture entitled *Discovering Puerto Rico*.

We also hosted several conferences and talks on the impact of mining in various towns. The first such event took place outside of Adjuntas and was led by Attorney Noemilda Vélez of The Bar Association of Puerto Rico. Tinti Deyá, Eduardo García, and I (Alexis Massol González) participated. That night, we presented a documentary in Super-8 format, which, although it jumped between topics, conveyed the opinions of campesinos about the mining issue. Josie Ballester, our graphic artist and the producer of the documentary, presented that night, along with important local figures from the Vegas Abajo, Vegas Arriba, Pellejas, and Tanamá neighborhoods. At the end of the screening, don Juan Rivera declared that, if we allowed the mining to proceed, "we would all have to go to Hell." The jíbaro spoke, the audience understood and erupted in a standing ovation.

Upon returning to Adjuntas, I told the people who ran the workshops about an experience that I had that day:

> It so happened that I arrived with Tinti at don Juan Antonio Corretejer's home at three in the afternoon. We had been talking for a while, when doña Consuelo scolded don Juan and told me to lie down in his bedroom. She said with much love and tenderness that I should rest before the conference. I rested in that other room, a humble and sacred place. There, I felt that they offered me more than just physical rest. I felt energies accumulated around the old desk and the antique typewriter where the poet wrote the immortal "Oubau Moin," later turned by Lucecita Benítez and Roy Brown into the hymn that people sing today. My eyes traveled across the walls, and I was impacted by the posters on different topics and the bookcases full of books of wisdom. The black beret, hanging from the back of a chair that was a beautiful brown color, transported me to another intimate world that I had admired so much from the outside. And if you

allow me to jump to the present, I will tell you that this black
beret, a gift from my poet friend, can be found at the entrance
to the house whose owner is the town of Adjuntas, Puerto Rico.

We continued the educational and organizational work in
Maunabo, Isabela, the Ciudad Universitaria in Trujillo Alto, the
Maragüez neighborhood in Ponce, the Catholic University of
Ponce, the Colegio San Miguel in Utuado, and the University
of Puerto Rico campuses in Río Piedras and in Fajardo. In public housing centers, we screened films, including *El Salvador* and
Taíno Heritage. We also appeared on radio programs at WPAB and
WISO in Ponce, and WKAQ in San Juan. Everywhere we visited,
people would point to us and say, "Those are the ones who stand
against the mines." We had begun the process of what sociologist
Alain Touraine calls the principle of identity. We carried out these
early activities to defend our natural resources and protect both
environmental and human rights. We did this, as Vivian Mattei
reported in a piece for *La Voz del Sur,* "with a vision of the world
worthy of [Eugenio María de] Hostos, a pamphlet of Corretjer's
poetry in hand, and plantain stains on our shirts."

PLAN 2020

Plan 2020 lays out the government's strategic planning for Puerto
Rico from the year 1980 to 2020. It consists of various federal
and Puerto Rican government documents, along with a map that
graphically illustrates the government's territorial plans through
2020. The document is formally titled *Master Plan for Puerto Rico
1980-2020,* and was financed by the United States Department of
Housing and Urban Development. Divided into six major areas,
the Plan called for the following:

Natural Resources: reserve 37,000 acres of land in the central
    part of the island for open pit mining of copper, gold, sil-

ver, molybdenum, and zinc in the municipalities of Adjuntas, Utuado, Lares, and Jayuya.

Infrastructure: construction of a new highway from Ponce, through Adjuntas and Utuado, to Arecibo, for access to the areas zoned for mining. In addition, the Plan provides for the development of several dams in the neighborhoods of Maragüez and Tibes in Ponce, with the aim of supplying the enormous amounts of water necessary for the mines, along with cheap energy. The Plan also provides for building coal-fired power plants, water treatment plants, and water mains throughout the island, including a section of a Northern Super Aqueduct.

Industry: construction of eleven industrial super parks, located in places with access to seaports, airports, water resources, energy resources, solid waste disposal facilities, highways, etc.

Military: maintain the military zones in Vieques, Culebra, Roosevelt Roads in Ceiba, Ramey Base in Aguadilla, Camp Santiago in Salinas, and other federally controlled areas. In total, 15% of the national territory is used for military purposes.

Agriculture: reserve lands with agricultural potential, mostly in the coastal plains. No lands in the central or west parts of the island were designated for agricultural development because of the priority given to mining.

Urban Development: identifies areas of expected urban development driven by population growth.

The Plan also included a number of supplemental materials, such as a Comprehensive Water Quality Management Plan for Puerto Rico (1970–2020); and a report titled *Island-Wide Water Supply Study* (1980), by the United States Army Corps of Engineers. The first calls for the construction of dams in the Maragüez and Tibes neighborhoods in Ponce, among other construction plans. It specifies how to avoid flooding, describes the impacts on the metal industry, and proposes a water transmission pipeline that would circle the Island, including the section known today as the Northern Superaqueduct. Plan 2020 alerted us to the government's determination to expand mining, and confirmed that, this time, and in contrast to past decades, the matter was truly decided. We doubled down by organizing more conferences, discussions, and meetings to connect the dots between Plan 2020 and the seemingly isolated environmental issues of different neighborhoods. Thanks to these events, we were able to build a network with other activist groups focused on cases dealing with regional treatment plants, industrial parks, solid waste facilities, dams, highways, and coal-fired power plant proposals in Yabucoa, Mayagüez, Ceiba, Humacao, Arecibo, Barceloneta, Ponce, and other municipalities.

In 1982 we increased our media presence by appearing on radio shows at WPAB in Ponce, WFKE in Yauco, a station in Fajardo, and TV Channel 7. We held conferences at the University of Puerto Rico in Mayagüez, the Los Caobos neighborhood in Ponce, the Labor Institute of Union Education (ILES) in Mayagüez, the Prisa green housing development group, and forums in Utuado, Maunabo, Isabela, and at the Interamerican University in Arecibo. We knew that organizing only at the local community level would not be enough to stop the mines. What was still missing to overcome the threat of mining was the participation by more sectors at the national level. During this process, we came to be known as the "anti-mining people," and also as the "folks working with Plan 2020." Our names were not important; what was important was that people were noticing and remembering us by the issues we were raising. The struggle was gaining strength.

MARAGÜEZ: EMBRACING COMMUNITIES IN THEIR STRUGGLES

In 1982, we began offering technical and other assistance to a group of residents in Ponce's Maragüez neighborhood. They had solicited support in their fight against the construction of a dam that would eliminate the old neighborhood, displacing the entire community by destroying the homes of 430 families. This issue led us to study Plan 2020 in more in depth. In our research, we had found an important document from the United States Army Corps of Engineers titled *Island-Wide Water Supply Study,* dated September of 1980. The document proposed the comprehensive development of the water supply infrastructure for all of Puerto Rico. It included the construction of the largest dam complexes in the Caribbean, one in the Maragüez neighborhood and another in Tibes, both in the municipality of Ponce and both now have been constructed. Within the construction blueprints we found a water supply pipeline that would go from the dams to the beach of Guayanilla, and continue on to the future site of the Commonwealth Oil Refining Company (CORCO), on land that mining companies had already bought. The proposed mining plan required large supplies of water and foresaw the use of an already existing deep-water seaport to export the refined minerals. The *Island-Wide Water Supply Study* provided for the construction of a water pipeline to encircle the Island and supply the 11 industrial superparks proposed in Plan 2020. The primary aim was to supply water to industries that had begun to set up throughout the island in response to a 1974 federal law, popularly known as Section 936, that allowed profits from U.S. businesses who set up shop in Puerto Rico to operate tax-free. These included chemical plants and manufacturers of electronics and pharmaceuticals, all major consumers of water. The portion of the water pipeline known as the *Superaqueduct of the North* began construction in 1998 and was finished in September of 2000.

Our interest in the mining situation got us involved in the local struggle against the dam in Maragüez. In terms of lessons learned, we were able to closely study the implementation of Plan 2020 as a model of what large interests favored for the economic development for Puerto Rico. Similarly, we better understood that Plan 2020 included coal-fired power plants to produce cheap energy and the construction of a highway to access the mining zone.

On March 13, 14, and 15, 1982, we celebrated a day of solidarity for Ma-ra-güez, in which the usual team from Mapeyé–Américo Boschetti, Tere Marichal, Noel Hernández and a group of artisans–participated. We held a conference entitled *Plan 2020 and Mining*, to dispel confusion about the impacts of mining and to refute the false narrative that the mining industry was promoting, namely, that the main purpose of the dam was to supply potable water to the south of the country. We were proven right when the dam was finished in 1995, and despite the severe drought that year, water was so scarce for private citizens in the south of the island that the government had to make an emergency call for bids for a pipeline to connect the Maragüez Dam to the water distribution system operated by the Puerto Rico Aqueduct and Sewer Authority. We worked in solidarity with the Maragüez community, organizing rallies, picket lines, and radio and television programs in which we discussed the rich archeological history that the dams threatened to destroy. One week, Channel 2 transmitted a series of reports that covered the fight against the dam and the mines. The police and the FBI were quick to brutally repress the movement: they used threats and intimidation tactics to instill fear and even suspended water and electricity for weeks. Bribery was another tactic: community members regularly received large cash offers for their properties. In the end, 430 families were evicted from their homes after two years of intense struggle. Valiant men and women resisted until the final moment. Nevertheless, the dam was built and Maragüez, one of the oldest communities in Ponce, was soon engulfed in water.

It's worth noting that support from the south and other parts of the island for the people of Maragüez was lackluster. The official argument for building the two dams was that the region needed water supply infrastructure. That was enough to convince many people to look the other way. We learned from this experience that whenever the governments of Puerto Rico and the United States work together to push for a project that will harm Puerto Ricans, successful resistance requires not only a strong and combative community organization, but also solidarity and support at the national level. We did have a combination of these factors going for us in several other more successful campaigns. These included blocking the construction of a Voice of America radio station in Cabo Rojo, the Congentrix Coal Plant in Mayagüez, and the Club Med in Bahía Ballena, Guánica. Many distinguished leaders lead these struggles, including don Efrén Pérez, who went on to become a key anti-mining activist and founder of the Caborrojeño Pro-Health and Environment Committee.

VILLA SIN MIEDO

In 1982, we read in the news that the government had ordered the eviction of a group of people who had been living in an informal settlement without land titles near the town of Carolina. They resisted, declaring themselves the community of Villa Sin Miedo (Fearless Village). Inspired by their story, we wanted to learn more. We invited them to Adjuntas to participate in an event on April 2, 1982 in the town plaza. Later, they invited us to visit the Villa. With great kindness, they shared their unforgettable community project with us. By themselves, they had built streets, a cultural center, a church, an electric lighting system, and a water and sewage system. They were, in a true sense, an independent and self-governing community. At the highest point of the Villa, they had built a look-out post to keep an eye out for signs of incoming police forces coming to evict them. The Puerto Rican flag flew atop it. At the look-out post, we asked them what we could contribute to their cause and, in response to their request, we returned with seeds for plantains, bananas, and vegetables. We also brought them an old plow along with donations from an event that we had jointly held in the plaza of Adjuntas. Less than a month later, we would watch with tears in our eyes as a brutal scene unfolded on television: the Villa destroyed, and the people who had hosted us evicted, their houses ablaze amid the sounds of gunfire. We were witnessing the destruction of an exemplary initiative, unique in the history of Puerto Rico, of a community land reclamation project that allowed the poor to live with dignity.

Journalist Wilda Rodríguez described the eviction of Villa Sin Miedo in the newspaper *El Nuevo Día,* May 19, 1982:

> At 11:15 in the morning, Police officers ripped down the flag of Puerto Rico from the look-out post of Villa Sin Miedo and raised their own shock-troopers flag to proclaim their victory in evicting the Villa's inhabitants after just over an hour of skirmishes. A contingent of police entered through the back of the Villa, delivering blows and spreading teargas as they dragged a caravan of children, adults, and elderly people to the entrance of the Villa, where another police contingent awaited them.

This experience taught us the lesson that communities need to understand and situate their struggles within the larger political and economic context. Otherwise, they risk mobilizing successfully to solve an immediate problem, only to see their organizational strength disappear once the immediate problem is solved. Instead, communities should always seek to connect their struggles with other struggles elsewhere and to build solidarity across their networks. Often, the government and politicians will wait until the very last minute to act in order to calm people down and dispel discontent. They might agree to pave unpaved streets, or to provide water and basic supplies to first responders in an emergency. But if communities don't have a long-term organizing strategy, they are vulnerable to tactics like these that aim to shut down movements.

Villa Sin Miedo broke with the established order and outdated values and institutions; the attack on it was an opening for more people to question the government and its structures of political, economic, and ideological domination. The assault on the town empowered more critical and creative people to imagine a different world without these constraints. The people of Villa Sin Miedo were an affront to the values of obedience, discipline, and subordination, all of which are tools employed by the system to create "law-abiding" men and women who will be docile. After the attack, I reflected at length. The right strategy and tactics for community-led struggles depend on the issue at hand. Communities engaged in struggle and resistance need to identify the true adversary so as not to confuse their aims. Some community struggles, such as Villa Sin Miedo, need broad solidarity from the Puerto Rican people, and sometimes even international support. This type of broad-based strategy could be the key to removing the United States Navy from Vieques, and to resisting their plans to install radar systems in Vieques and Lajas.

THE STRUGGLE INTENSIFIES

We spent much of 1982 supporting the struggles of Maragüez and Villa Sin Miedo, and resisting Plan 2020 nationally, but we did not abandon our local work. One of our major activities in Adjuntas that year was to organize and hold public hearings on mining in the Adjuntas municipal building. These hearings were co-sponsored by a coalition of religious groups in the United States and Puerto Rico, and featured more than twenty speakers, including ministers and priests from the island and the United States. We also reorganized our canvassing teams, which continued visiting residents in different neighborhoods, educating and collecting signatures in opposition to mining. These personal interactions generated more trust as people got to know us. We made good friends throughout the town as we worked to wake up this land of the "Sleeping Giant," as Adjuntas is popularly known because of the silhouette of a mountain to the southeast of town.

Engineers from Adjuntas who had participated in the Arts and Culture Workshop went to national and international conferences, gathering more information to strengthen our arguments against mining while sharing our story more widely outside of Puerto Rico. The engineer Eduardo García, for example, presented to the United Nations Special Committee on Decolonization on August 2, 1982. On September 18, 1982, I participated in a Forum on Mining at the University of Puerto Rico at Utuado, alongside Dr. Neftalí García and attorney Víctor Agrait from the organization Misión Industrial. Agrait had long campaigned against mining, and his expertise was valuable to our team. The first publication to come out of the Arts and Culture Workshop was a book that I wrote entitled *De la deformación a la destrucción* (From Deformation to Destruction).

Also in 1982, we set out to find the grave of the national hero Joaquín Parilla, a key leader of the *Grito de Lares,* the opening salvo of the Puerto Rican independence struggle against the Spanish Empire in 1868. The stories that had been passed down to us orally led us to a site marked by a wooden cross. Using documents we obtained from the library of the University of Puerto Rico, and with the help of Dr. Ricardo Alegría, we finally found the grave after multiple attempts in Adjuntas, Peñuelas, and Guayanilla: it was covered in limestone and sand. We could hear the immortal words of Parilla reverberating within us: "Joaquín Parilla never surrenders!" These words, uttered while under siege by Spanish militias, is part of our legacy, and visiting Parilla's grave reinvigorated our hope for a better future.

We rounded out the year with a second kite festival and a *Dialogue with Patriots* in the Adjuntas public square, featuring legendary figures of the Puerto Rican independence movement like Rafael Cancel Miranda, Irvin Flores, and Oscar Collazo. These events, along with all the other experiences that we had in the early 1980s, built the foundations of the Arts and Culture Workshop; though we were still in our early stages as an organization and movement, the State was already organizing its repressive forces against us. A sympathetic policeman from the southern part of the island informed us that the Workshop had been infiltrated. Thanks to his tip, we managed to identify and expel a high school student known as Prietri, who had been passing information on all our activities to the federal government for a few bucks. We later identified him in declassified files of the Intelligence Division, Puerto Rico Police as informant # 332-H3. Consequently, while we did not know what the future might still hold for us, one thing was clear: the spirit of the Puerto Rican struggle, embodied by leaders like Corretjer and the heroes who joined us in the square for our event, was now part of our basic makeup as an organization.

THE DIASPORA CAMPAIGN

As the campaign grew, we sought and found solidarity and support for our struggle among the many local communities of the Puerto Rican diaspora in the United States. We went on a three-week anti-mining tour with stops in New York, New Jersey, Chicago, Michigan, Detroit, San Francisco, Los Angeles, and Colorado. We visited more than twenty universities and cultural centers and made appearances on various television and radio programs. In Washington, D.C., we gave a presentation at a public hearing sponsored by religious leaders. For us, it was a huge learning experience. We learned about the poverty and discrimination faced by Puerto Ricans in the diaspora, and about the good will and support that our compatriots in the United States held for us. My wife Tinti and I presented separately in these educational events, and together at the United Nations. The main themes of our United States tour were the Plan 2020 and the many adverse impacts of mining. It was sponsored by the Chicago Cultural Center, and by universities and Hispanic groups that stood in solidarity with us. We saw we had attracted attention when the United States Mining Bureau mentioned the Adjuntas Arts and Culture Workshop in one of its bulletins.

Throughout 1983 we continued to carry out different activities in Adjuntas, including poetry recitals with Pedro Zervigón and Américo Boschetti, a film festival at the local school and in the plaza, a conference at the University of Puerto Rico in Mayagüez, another conference sponsored by the Student Council at the Center for Advanced Studies of Puerto Rico and the Caribbean in Old San Juan, and, at year's end, a women's volleyball tournament. Although national and U.S. support was growing, we felt we still had a long way to go at home in Adjuntas. We could also see that the government and the mining companies were already taking steps to begin extracting minerals. As we moved through this process, we learned how complex it is to organize a community in struggle around specific demands. It requires careful strategic planning and execution, rather than merely improvising and acting as opportunities arise. It is naive to think that your adversaries are acting in good faith. As Manuel Zeno Gandía put it in his unforgettable novel, *La charca,* "One cannot solve arduous problems with lyrical outbursts, just as one cannot tunnel through mountains with a living room fan."

THE THREAT OF MINING GROWS

The first three years had taught us a lot. We came to understand that it would not be easy to stop mining from happening. We knew that the United States and Puerto Rican governments were using all of their political power to promote mining as a matter of economic development. After twenty years of planning, AMAX and Kennecott had purchased the lands where the two biggest mineral deposits were located. They were getting ready to start mining. The threat was closer than ever. The Adjuntas Arts and Culture Workshop researched more and found documents and agreements that corroborated that the companies were moving forward. The Comprehensive Development Plan of the Governor's Office included mining in Puerto Rico as a public policy priority. The United

States Bureau of Mines, in an official document dated January 13, 1982, recommended large-scale mining and the establishment of a refinery and smelter system on the island. The 1983 budget for the Mineral Development Corporation earmarked $100,000 to start preparing its Statement on Environmental Impact. The Puerto Rico Planning Board, which had identified 37,000 acres for mining, began denying construction permits to the smallholder farmers who owned those plots. Even the Catholic Church was barred from building a new church in the Vegas Arriba neighborhood of Adjuntas. Confidential information from the highest levels of government indicated that approval of the Plan was just around the corner. In addition, local mayors, the governor, legislators, the Puerto Rico Medical Association, other national institutions, and some well-known people from Adjuntas were speaking openly in favor of mining. Everything seemed to be carefully orchestrated.

We felt the gravity of the challenge and the weight of our historical responsibility. We understood that once mining began and millions of dollars were invested in mining infrastructure, the process would be irreversible; nothing would stop their pursuit of profit. We knew that this would mark the beginning of the destruction of the land, our territory, and even our nation: without a territory suitable for collective living, the Puerto Rican homeland would die. We knew that the United States had no intention of guiding Puerto Rico towards statehood or an improved Commonwealth (ELA), let alone to status as an independent republic. Instead, they meant to turn Puerto Rico into a consumer society fully dependent on the United States, a kind of extractive "reservation" with all its cultural expressions geared towards the enjoyment of tourists, as happened in Hawaiʻi . Puerto Ricans would become strangers in their own land. Facing this harsh reality was overwhelming to us at first. But instead of singing a Borinquen lament, we began a process of intense reflection about what to do to win the people's hearts so that they would act to defend their future. We urgently needed to find a locally organized alternative if we were to have any hope of success.

CHAPTER 3

PUERTO RICAN CULTURE

A Tool of Resistance

The second anti-mining campaign drew large crowds thanks to *The Motherland Concert*, a major cultural event featuring talent from Adjuntas. September 17–21, 1984.

WHAT IS TO BE DONE, AND HOW?

We dedicated most of 1983 to conducting an in-depth analysis of what to do next and how to do it. Tinti, Noemilda, Brunilda García, Ileana Carrión, and I worked on this with fierce passion. The results of our labor came to define the trajectory of our organization, then known as the *Taller de Arte y Cultura de Adjuntas,* the Adjuntas Arts and Culture Workshop. Our analysis showed that the government and the mining companies had become more uncompromising than ever in their commitment to exploit our copper, gold, and silver deposits. Although most of the town opposed the mining projects, the local people demonstrated a certain level of apathy and unwillingness to get involved in the conflict. Fear, the product of a history of oppression and intimidation, weighed on Adjuntas as much as it did on the rest of Puerto Rico. The Adjuntas Arts and Culture Workshop was generally viewed sympathetically as a pro-independence revolutionary group ready to do what needed to be done. Nevertheless, it was clear that the Workshop had not generated the wide base of community support that the circumstances required. Our analysis revealed that there was a disconnect between everyday people, the Workshop, and the struggle. How to shorten the distance between ordinary citizens and the Workshop had proved to be a challenge. Clearly, we needed a new strategy, and we had our breakthrough when we discovered that Puerto Rican culture could be employed as a tool of resistance.

We decided our next step would be to stage a large cultural event with resources and talent from Adjuntas, and we called it *The Motherland Within.* To bring the idea to life, we organized ourselves according to our skills and areas of interest and we started various working groups, or commissions. These included commissions for artisans, for traditional dance among the young people, for folk singers and musicians, for agriculture, and for a study of mining. We also organized an artist group of women called Las Marianas, composed of wives, mothers, and allies of our struggle. We grew in number and in the diversity of our political views, opinions, and ideas about life. We established a new, rich, and complex organizing body with the immediate objective of stopping the mines. On October 4, 1983, the Artists' Commission met. Folk singers, musicians, and artists of all kinds agreed to participate in the defense of our shared territory. On November 12, a much larger meeting took place with members from all the commissions and all the collaborators in the growing Adjuntas Arts and Culture Workshop. The dialogue about *what to do and how* prepared us to start 1984 with plenty of enthusiasm. *The Motherland Within* would serve as both cultural expression and artistic ammunition. Whether this combination of knowledge, culture, and community would be effective had yet to be proven.

THE MOTHERLAND WITHIN

The Motherland Within Concert (*Concierto Patria Adentro*) became a cultural production that brought together all the commissions and working groups. Brunilda García and Ramón Calderín worked as the designers, consultants, and collaborators that brought the show to life. With no previous experience in theater, we wrote the script together. The production included two narrators, three folk singers, five musicians, and six members of the youth folk-dance group. The light technician, the stagehand, the stage manager, and the sound engineer were integral members of the team. One person oversaw the projection of large images of our country's wealth of natural beauty, culture and humanity; these slides were synced to the narration and lyrics of the songs. I prepared a short talk about Plan 2020 and the mining industry for the show's intermission. Some volunteers prepared the dressing room, while others readied a lighting system using galvanized tubes, large cans with a hole cut out in them and multicolored lightbulbs. This was a completely new experience for us, a new form of learning, and a different way to fight. The artisans stepped into the limelight to showcase their crafts and make themselves known to the community. Culture, along with learning, was the central focus.

We began rehearsals and meetings. Brunilda and the dancers held several workshops on physical expression and heel toe dance techniques. Rosa Meneses Albizu, the granddaughter of Puerto Rican independence movement hero don Pedro Albizu Campos and then a member of the National Ballet of Cuba, instructed the group, as did Tere Marichal. Sometimes we had to go back and make changes to the script to improve it or go out into the countryside and take more photos for the slideshow. It took a lot of effort to put on this production and to bring together more than thirty amateurs around one goal—not to mention organizing all the volunteers who built the stage, did the publicity, and coordinated the events. Puerto Rican culture was the artistic tool we had been missing to help us frame our struggle as one of national affirmation.

Mounting the production raised our self-esteem and clarified who we were and who we wanted to be. This was the key: we had to value ourselves first to be able to fight with a desire to win. Our slogan was: "Sí a la vida, no a las minas" (Yes to Life, No to Mining.) We learned that happiness is in the fight itself and that the best way to speak is with actions. Noemilda and Tinti; Sandra, Nomaris, and Yomaira; along with Alexito, Curi, Arturo and Ariel, all filled important roles working with our neighbors on Water Street (including María and Tita). Fonso Vélez Massol developed his photography skills; he was also the light technician and grew increasingly more involved. Salvador Acevedo and "el Corso" were the most active of the artisans. And occasionally, musicians and folk singers—Tony and Sixto Ostolaza, the Badea Brothers, el Indio, Casimiro Miró, Aniel Irizarry, and Tata Ramos—energized the group with their songs. It was not easy to find harmony among people with so many differing political voices without losing the specific character of each individual. Sometimes participants would move away from the group a bit, but they would typically return. The concept of *unity* is often over-emphasized in social movements. We managed to find unity without speaking, and despite our differences, by working together to beat the mining industry without compromising our fundamental beliefs.

The debut performance of *The Motherland Within* took place on February 25, 1984, at the San Joaquín High School in Adjuntas in front of a full house. When it was over, no one wanted to leave, and instead stayed to shower the performers with hugs and praise. Artisans shared some of their works as gifts. A new chapter had begun. The distance between the people and those who were fighting for their interests started to shrink. Every member of the Workshop became a leader. From that day on we sang, taking our message to different places, affirming our identity, valuing what we had, and fighting to defend it. People began to request performances of *The Motherland Within*, and we obliged that same year with a presentation at the Fishermen's festival in Vieques, held in opposition to the presence on the island of United States Marines. Truthfully, I don't remember how we transported ourselves from Adjuntas to Fajardo and then on the ferry to Vieques and back with our contingent of dreamers. It seemed like magic or a miracle. Looking at the photos now, I see distinct moments of the trip filled with beautiful, smiling faces full of life. As we approached Vieques, we heard a powerful voice singing in the distance, "Barlovento, amarra el perro y suelta el viento…" (Windward side of the boat, tie up the dog and release the wind). It was Andrés "El Jíbaro" Jiménez, who later joined our team. In the following months we performed *The Motherland Within* throughout Puerto Rico: at an homage to the immortal bolero singer Davilita in an unforgettable display sponsored by the Bayamón Teachers' Federation; at the University of Puerto Rico in Río Piedras; and for the Conference for the National Affirmation of the Social Sciences, in an event organized by Doctor Luis Nieves Falcón, who also later joined our group. Everywhere we went, the show was a success, the attendance was solid, and we met people who later became important collaborators with the

Workshop. All the events were free of charge, with artists contributing voluntarily to defend their country. Between concerts we continued to offer conferences on Plan 2020 and the Mining Industry. We presented at the University of Puerto Rico campuses in Humacao, Río Piedras, and Aguadilla. We also made presentations to the medical students at the Catholic University in Ponce, to the teachers in the Teachers' Federation in Morovis, at the Santa Rita High School in Bayamón, at the University of Puerto Rico Law School, and to a religious group in Ceiba that included the celebrated patriot Doña Isabelita Rosado.

WORK CONTINUES AT THE LOCAL LEVEL

Throughout 1984, we continued to evolve productively at the local level thanks to a lot of dedication and collective effort. The presence of the Workshop grew as word spread and we began to accept invitations to perform at schools, hospitals, and at the Adjuntas *Centro para Envejecientes* (Center for the Aging), where the attendees declared themselves to be in opposition to mining. At the Rafael Aparicio Jiménez Middle School, we curated an exhibition of works by artist Miguel Ángel Guzmán, which dealt with the theme of mining and was titled *Canto a la Naturaleza* (A Hymn to Nature). At that same school, we organized a film festival and a talk about the mining industry given by Arturo Massol, one of our members, to his group of seventh grade students. Doors that were once closed now opened to us. For the first time, the Kite Festival that we had been putting on for years, drew in a large crowd. More than 300 people including more than fifty kite flyers came to the event. The most common kite themes were the Puerto Rican flag, provincial figures, and designs evoking the mining industry. Our kite was in support of Puerto Rican prisoners of war. During an earlier visit to Chicago, we had met Luz and Alicia Rodríguez, two jailed patriots. At the Kite Festival, the sisters' faces seemed to fly free in the Adjuntas sky.

Little by little, we persuaded the town to our way of thinking and doing things. Together with religious groups, hospitals, and regular citizens, we began a campaign against the noise produced by cars with loudspeakers during electoral campaigns. This increased our range of action. The political parties were driving people crazy with constant noise day and night. "The truth doesn't shout," became our motto. We gathered petitions, hung banners, passed out bulletins, and introduced an ordinance which the Municipal Assembly passed in its entirety. The community saw that we succeeded in lessening the noise, proving our intention of working in their best interests. To round out the year and prepare for the next stage of resistance to the mining industry, the Workshop published my book *Plan 2020 and Mining Industry Exploitation,* and *The Motherland Within* was performed in the neighborhoods near the mining sites.

In September 1984 we held our biggest production to date, a weeklong festival of cultural events in support of our anti-mining struggle. On the first day, we celebrated the reopening of the Joaquín Parrilla Gallery at its new location. Dr. Ricardo Cordero from Adjuntas, who was Pedro Albizu Campos' doctor, unveiled the new space. An exhibit of paintings by Rafael Rivera Rosa and a poetry recital by our own Brunilda García were the highlights of the night. Filled with such remarkable people, the small venue felt much bigger than it really was. On the second day, we held a symposium on the mining industry in the town plaza, featuring speakers Juan Antonio Corretjer, Dr. Luis Nieves Falcón, law student at the University of Puerto Rico José Amundaray, and me. This was followed by a recital of Afro-Puerto Rican poetry and a concert by Adjuntas troubadours. During the following days we held performances of *The Motherland Within* and a National Concert featuring several artists. We closed on the last day with singer Andrés "El Jíbaro" Jiménez and his band. The week had been a major success. There were lots of people in attendance, and there was a visible shift in in the size and composition of the audience. It was completely different from our first major event in that same plaza, back in September 1981 with its attendance of one. We felt that our hard work was paying off. Little by little we were doing away with the separation between us and the people of Adjuntas. However, we were not about to rest on our laurels; we knew that we had to keep working if we wanted to win against the powerful mining industry. With that thought in our minds, we finished 1984, a year full of hope, hard work and accomplishments, with a Celebration of Fellowship at the covered basketball court of Adjuntas on the December 16, 1984.

PLAN 2020 AND MINING INDUSTRY EXPLOITATION

Community organizing sometimes led to pleasant surprises. My book *Plan 2020 and Mining Industry Exploitation* began to be used at the University of Puerto Rico in Río Piedras, and our talks on campus started to fill amphitheaters. In return, students and university professors visited us in Adjuntas in search of more information and to offer their support in solidarity with the movement. Students began to write their masters theses and doctoral dissertations in collaboration with us; the first of these was a student from the School of Social Work at the University of Puerto Rico in Río Piedras. This led to new collaborations, more support, and much learning. On May 9, 1985, Dr. Luis Nieves Falcón hosted the presentation of my book at the Aboy House in San Juan, and more people started to invite us to give our talk. We did, at the University of Puerto Rico in Ponce, in Ciales, to religious groups in Vieques, and at the Ponce Medical School where a student wrote a thesis on the implications of mining to public health. The findings of his thesis reaffirmed the urgency of our fight and lent further credibility to the plans we had made. Our presence was also felt at the national level. The Workshop helped with a report I presented at the First Meeting of Environmental Organizations in Ponce. We participated in two big marches: one in defense of El Yunque

National Forest, which was threatened by the planned felling of 6000 trees; and another against nuclear arms, on June 9 in Ceiba. We also were invited to speak on several radio programs in support the campaign, which was a good way to maintain contact with everybody living in and around Adjuntas.

GROWING FROM WITHIN

1985 saw many changes to the way the Workshop functioned and to overall levels of participation. It also saw the birth of a new project of great significance to Puerto Rico that I describe in the next chapter. For these reasons, we can describe 1985 as the year the organization *grew from within*. The rehearsals and meetings for *The Motherland Within* continued unabated. On March 23, we presented the program in Vegas Abajo, an anti-mining neighborhood. Some 200 people attended, a resounding success and a strengthening of our anti-mining campaign. We held the fifth Kite Festival on March 30 and dedicated it to the memory of our dear musician friend from Adjuntas, Chelo Román. On May 11, we celebrated Puerto Rican Mother's Day in the covered basketball court. It turned out to be another encouraging success, featuring participants from every one of the commissions in our Workshop, as well as members of two newly founded groups, the anti-mining chapter of Vegas Abajo, and the Adjuntas Student Democratic Front. There was music, poetry, a raffle, presents, and flowers for all the women in attendance. Finally, we presented a commemorative plaque to the organizer of the Kite Festival, Alfonso Vélez, and a donation to a family who had lost their home on Water Street to fire.

AN INFRACTION OF THE LAW

One problem we cannot overlook is institutional oppression of the kind that is designed to intimidate, punish, or slow efforts that oppose the interests of the State and the entrenched economic and political powers. We had by that time become a real threat to those interests. We were never blind to this fact and, in fact, we lived it in our own flesh. Since 1984, Secret Police had been assigned to constantly monitor us and the events we organized. They followed us to meetings we held in other towns and carried out the sad assignment of visiting the homes of our dance group members, folk singers, musicians, artists, and collaborators to intimidate them. We only found out about the harassment when nobody came to a meeting. Once we found out why no one had shown up, we had to start all over to convince them to return. It was a constant struggle to put on the performance of *Motherland Within* during this period. Elsewhere, teachers who were part of our organization were reassigned to lesser jobs in the school system with the aim of intimidating them, scaring other members, and discouraging the older students from joining our cause. They searched our houses and even slaughtered animals on our properties. Wherever we went, they went there, too. When returning from events outside of town, a car would follow us all the way back to Adjuntas, even to our homes. The partial release of secret files drawn up by the Police Intelligence Division provides evidence of the surveillance we were under. Several informants infiltrated the Workshop to do harm to our fight to save the water, the earth, the air, and our shared resources by preventing the exploitation of the mining deposits. For a few bucks, Rodríguez, Natal, Pietri, and someone called Antonmarchi (332-H-2), all sold their souls. Their collaboration with the government and mining interests put our lives in grave danger. We lived under constant threat.

CHAPTER 4

THE BIRTH OF CASA PUEBLO

A silkscreen poster donated by artist Antonio
Maldonado helped raise funds for the house
that became the headquarters of Casa Pueblo. June 1985.

A HOUSE OWNED BY THE PEOPLE

Learning through direct experience revealed the secret of what would be our next step. We needed to find a permanent home. Of course, it was one thing to hear what our conscience was telling us to do, and another to do it. But just as in love, one small arrow was all it took to get us started.

One afternoon in 1985, Tinti and I walked past a large, abandoned house in Adjuntas. Vines and flowering plants covered it, as untended as the house itself. Nevertheless, it was imposing and beautiful. I remembered the lovely girl who lived there during the summertime when I was a child. But this time as I walked by, it occurred to me that we could acquire it and make it the permanent home of our community organization, a base from which we could continue the fight of the last five years against the mines. A utopia, the first of many to come. As a group, we discussed the reasonableness of the idea and the difficulties of pulling it off. After a silence, I said, "Is dreaming not allowed? Where is our sense of hope?" I thought that a sense of helplessness and dismay should not hold us back. So, with your permission dear reader, I will tell you a story that, although it may seem made up, is not only true, but also allowed us to start writing a history that now looks like it will have no end.

After several failed attempts to set up a meeting, the owner of the house finally agreed to talk with me about the price and condition of the property. She turned out to be the same young woman I knew from the summers of my youth: Isabelita Espina Mattei. I asked for the sale price. "One hundred thousand," she said firmly. "But the house is falling apart," I said, starting the negotiation. Trying to bring the number down, I added, "We will convert it into an independent cultural center that will bring glory to the people of Adjuntas." Right away she responded, "In that case, I'll give it to you for $90,000." I understood her goodwill and she understood mine, so I kept negotiating. "We will build the Eugenio María de Hostos Library, it will have a shop of artisanal goods, and it will run on solar energy, and, in the back patio, there will be a lovely butter-fly sanctuary." With each additional detail that I shared about our vision she lowered the price another ten thousand dollars. When we reached 50,000 she said firmly, "I won't lower it any further. Let's sign the contract and finish this deal," said Isabelita, to whom we still owe infinite gratitude. Then came the hardest part, even more difficult than the first, but dreams give you the hope and the nerve to act. "It's just that, we don't have the money," I answered. Then, somewhat irritated, she asked, "What do you have?" "Only the will to make it happen," was my response. Generously, she gave us a period of six months to pay $25,000 and six more years to come up with the other half. "Deal," I replied happily. The members of the Workshop accepted the proposal and we embarked on a journey into the unknown.

It's one thing to stand up to the mining industry; it's quite another to finance an ambitious project starting with nothing. Desperate, I went with Josie Ballester to our congressman's office in Utuado to ask him for a donation. We came back buzzing with happiness after he gave us $25,000 from pork barrel funding. We had covered the first half of the payment and had six years to come up with the rest. We held our first meeting in the house on a rainy day, with umbrellas over our heads because the old zinc roof was leaking. Noé's leg fell through a hole in the floor of the living room. And then we started the meeting. We reviewed the economic plan to make sure there weren't any inconsistencies, and everyone accepted it. We also agreed to name the house *Casa Pueblo*. But the joy of having a permanent base from which to fight was abruptly cut short. Doña Martina asked to speak. She was a woman who did not know how to read or write, eked out a living by weeding lawns, collecting aluminum cans, and picking coffee. She lived on Water Street, one of the humblest parts of town. I thought with my elitist mentality, "What in the world could Doña Martina have to say?" "With that money they gave," she declared, "the politicians have bought Casa Pueblo forever." She was right and her few words produced a total and absolute silence, a long-lasting, deafening silence that stirred our conscience and led to a crossroads in our history. This was truly a master lesson for a community organization that values freedom and independence: *a house owned by the people.*

Determined to have a house owned by the people, we set out to pay back the $25,000 we had received from the congressman in six months' time, by the end of 1985. The first donations came from don Ricardo Alegría, Dr. Margot Arce de Vázquez, and the esteemed Adjuntas lawyer Minguín Quiless, among others. The great artist Antonio Maldonado made silk-screen prints of the facade of Casa Pueblo that, in addition to publicizing the organization, generated additional sources of income through sales of the image. Junior Cruz, the owner of the Funeral Home del Carmen, provided a suckling pig to make traditional pasteles. All this organizational work enabled us to grow in other ways, beyond protesting and fighting the mining industry and involving more people in our work. Our vision was starting to change. It was no longer monochromatic, but rather composed of many different stripes and shades of color.

A Night of Song and Poetry was the first fundraising event we held to help pay for the house. Rafi Escudero, Miguel Ángel Suárez, Brunilda García (from the group Cimarrón), María Gisela Rosado, Carlos and Carmencita, Tony Rivera and the Mapeyé collective, all donated their art. The event took place at the covered basketball court and the audience was large and enthusiastic. The town had come together to support a cause that they saw as their own. We finished the year with three performances: Mapeyé, in the neighborhood Garzas Juncos; Cimarrón, in Casa Pueblo; and the National Folkloric Ballet of the Autonomous University of Santo Domingo. For this meeting between the city of Santo Domingo and Adjuntas, the town of the Sleeping Giant, we contributed with a performance of *The Motherland Within.* In all these efforts, we worked toward establishing a center of resistance, and more importantly, a new home for Puerto Rican culture. In the end, we purchased the house with our own money and through our own efforts. Casa Pueblo was born free, thanks to Doña Martina's master class, and thanks to the women and men who organized to offer their support at the local and national levels, and even at the level of the community of Caribbean sister nations.

EUGENIO MARÍA DE HOSTOS IN CASA PUEBLO

Casa Pueblo quickly became an important tool in the fight against mining because it provided a physical space, a territory from which to defend our natural resources, culture, and people. Here we started a new process of identity formation. The house was always full of life and fighting spirit. With the constant stream of arrivals to this "house of communists," as the fearmongers called it, Casa Pueblo soon became a house not just of the people of Adjuntas, but of the whole nation. The Eugenio María de Hostos Library was the first project initiated inside the structure. We built the shelves, and afterward we asked ourselves how we would obtain the books to fill them. We planned an event where the participants would donate one book each and in just one day, the library was filled with literature about Puerto Rico and many other topics. We also participated in a radio program with Jannette Blasini of WPAB, to talk about our goals. It was a big surprise to hear one person say on a telephone call that they wanted to donate their copy of the complete set of works by Hostos and that we could come by their house to pick up the books after the show. That event, along with others that followed, pointed to a new discovery: the moral reserves and solidarity of the Puerto Rican people is of the kind that dispels pessimism and feelings of powerlessness.

On Sunday, January 12, 1988, we inaugurated the library and commemorated the 150th anniversary of the birth of Puerto Rican national hero: Eugenio María de Hostos. The front porch became a stage and we made space for the attendees on the front lawn.

Musician Andrés Jiménez and the Farmers' Workshop Group put on a concert, and Dr. José Ferrer Canales gave a brilliant speech in the afternoon. We also presented *Manifesto of a Town That Wants to Live*, a short document written with the help of poets Ché Meléndez and Ángela María Dávila, calling for an end to all mining in Puerto Rico. The manifesto was signed by everyone present and quickly became an important tool in our arsenal to stop the mining industry. From that day forward, we started collecting signatures. Everywhere we went–schools, meetings with religious and environmental groups, or conferences–we brought the Manifesto, and in less than six months, we had gathered over three thousand signatures.

With your permission, I'd like to recount a fond memory I have of the day of the library's inauguration. An old lady, face freckled and beaten by the sun, got up from her chair and walked right up to the speaker. He, in a most courteous and moving manner, stopped talking to help her climb the stairs and walk into Casa Pueblo. That woman, a faithful supporter of our cause, the red-haired daughter of Cándido from the Coabey neighborhood in Jayuya, and friend of Oscar Collazo, was Titi Ivel, my mother.

CHAPTER 5

THE FIRST STEPS TOWARD
SUSTAINABILITY

Tinti Deyá Díaz and Alexis Massol González process the first batch of Café
Madre Isla coffee. Summer of 1989.

SOWING SEEDS OF HOPE

Community self-governance is a proven and effective tool, but it is not necessarily equivalent to sustainability. If communities want to avoid projects that flourish briefly but soon fizzle and vanish, they must develop self-sustaining initiatives. By 1986, we had spent some time planning alternative projects in areas threatened by mining. On one occasion, a committee from the Arts and Culture Workshop visited farmer Jaimito Rullán Mayol. We asked him if we could use a plot of his land along Valdés Road to plant trees. We told him that we wanted to create a small model of what could become an alternative to mining by planting trees to establish sustainable forests and a timber enterprise. Without missing a beat, Mr. Mayol said "It's yours. I just donated three acres of land to you." We were perplexed to have had our wish granted so easily.

The struggle sometimes brings surprises. We named the ecological sustainability project *Planting Hope,* and celebrated its inauguration on Saturday, May 17 and Sunday, May 18, 1986. On Saturday, Puerto Rican singer-songwriter María Gisela Rosado performed at one of our events. It was a great joy for the audience and for us to experience solidarity with an artist committed to the *Casa* and the *Pueblo.* As usual, we also gave our *Mining and the 2020 Plan* presentation. On Sunday at eleven in the morning, we celebrated the planting of the national tree, the ceiba, in front of Casa Pueblo. It was a moving ceremony. We had asked people to bring a little bit of soil from their towns, and participants proceeded to scatter the soil around the newly planted tree. People from many towns and neighborhoods delivered their gift of Earth, chanting the names of the places the soil came from as they scattered it on the ground. These were offerings and blessings for a magical tree and a community that wanted to thrive.

"From Lares, altar of the homeland."
"From the tomb of our teacher, Pedro Albizu Campos."

"From the remains of the foundation of Juan and Consuelo's home in Guaynabo."

"From Ponce, the neighborhood of Guilarte de Adjuntas."

The lesson from this experience was that *music must accompany the process of struggle because it touches the hearts of the people in ways they never forget.* Then, we marched through town with our tree saplings in hand. It was a silent march, but our hearts were filled with determination to halt the deadly mining project. We were a liberation army, equipped not with rifles, but with trees to plant the hope of a village under siege by external forces. Oscar Collazo, stalwart fighter for Puerto Rican independence, humbly joined us in our march. Collazo was one of the Puerto Rican nationalist fighters who was arrested in 1950 for attempting to assassinate President Harry Truman at the Blair House in Washington D.C. His group was responding to Truman's "gag law," which criminalized any discussion about, or organizing around, Puerto Rican independence, including singing patriotic songs or displaying the Puerto Rican flag. As we approached the steep hill leading to the lands that Mr. Mayol had donated to our cause, Collazo spoke about how the struggle has multiple fronts, and all of them are important. The young organizers were eagerly awaiting us. Everything was well prepared. Newly opened trails led to holes that had already been dug throughout the steep terrain. Three hundred trees arrived to be planted, each with a tag that read:

> Planting Hope: A Pledge to Puerto Rico. This ticket is proof that you picked up this tree on Sunday, May 18, 1986, at 11:00 a.m. at Casa Pueblo. Your participation will be historic and an inspiration for the Puerto Rican people.

Through a speakerphone, Ariel gave the instructions. Each person stood in front of the hole in which they were going to plant their tree. They listened to instructions on how to remove the plastic bag and plant the tree. There were three hundred kids, teenagers, and adults standing in formation and in absolute silence. Ariel gave the order to start planting. In just three minutes, we planted 300 trees, completing the work. The moment stood as evidence of the power of a united village. All the signs pointed toward the possibility of a great community victory.

MADRE ISLA COFFEE

The *Madre Isla Coffee* project was born out of our discussions about community self-governance and the need to ensure continuity, sustainability, and permanent change. At one meeting, we talked about the possibility of developing a self-sufficient economy to sustain Casa Pueblo. After each person had shared their ideas and opinions, we still had not arrived at a clear consensus. Then, Freddie Abreu from Tanamá walked out onto the front porch and pointed toward the mountains. "There is the alternative," he said with certainty. Still, the rest of us saw nothing more than a green expanse. He insisted, but no one understood what he was getting at and we stood silently, like students in front of the headmaster. After we pushed him for an explanation, he said: "In the green expanse that you see is a great coffee plantation. High quality beans grown in shade produce the best coffee in the world." He continued, "From Puerto Rico, coffee used to be exported to the Vatican and other parts of Europe." He mentioned the ideal soil, altitude, and temperature to produce the highest-quality coffee. He spoke about other topics foreign to us, explaining the different varieties of coffee, and the differences between high quality *arabica* beans and other varieties. Madre Isla Coffee was born out of this illuminating discussion. Its name refers to *Madre Isla*, the title of a volume in the collected works by Eugenio María de Hostos, in which he argues for Puerto Ricans' right to be free, but also states that we must win that freedom with facts. And with facts, we started our work, looking to prove that a coffee crop was viable here and that it was a good option for making our community and work self-sustaining.

The first beans came from Millo Pérez's plantation. Cindo provided the toaster and mill, Danny Torres designed the label, and I designed the rustic packaging system. Tinti and Ariel, along with several others, filled the first jars. Our commitment to stop mining led us to affirm alternative, self-sufficient economic projects as a means of breaking our dependency. And so, Madre Isla Coffee began production in 1989. The following year, Tinti organized our *Artisanal Shop,* a gift shop in Casa Pueblo filled with hand-crafted products, as an additional building block in the economic solidarity project. All this was an organizational and educational milestone.

FINCA MADRE ISLA

This project represented a major step forward for our alternative model of living in community. It contained a positive vision of the future, and a concrete proposal that went beyond opposition to mining. We expended considerable effort to buy a three-acre plot of land in 1991, and we named it *Finca Madre Isla: Ecological, Community, and Cultural Tourism Project.* Even here, the specter of mining followed us. We found out that the region used to be known as The Mine because of the manganese extraction done there in the 1930s. Some craters and stores of minerals still dotted the landscape. At first, we cultivated coffee, citrus fruit, and passionfruit. Still, it took us three years to be able to pick the first golden bean of coffee. We learned how complicated agriculture is.

The coffee brigade members of Adjuntas and other towns came to support the project and ensure its viability. To promote community eco-tourism, we also constructed four rustic cabins and an activity center. From the start of the project, we relied on the solidarity of Mrs. Asunción, one of Hostos' daughters-in-law; and Tere de Hostos, a granddaughter of the author of *Madre Isla.* The Finca Madre Isla was also home to the patriot Antonio Cruz Colón until he built his own house elsewhere. As we built upon these great legacies, our project began to attract international attention. In 1991 and 1992, we received visitors from Germany, Holland, and the United States, as well as students from the Roberto Clemente Community Academy in Chicago and several universities. We also had visitors to the plantation from other town in Puerto Rico, including Salinas, Cataño, and Río Piedras.

All the while, we continued to carry out local advocacy work. We published and distributed *Tierra Adentro Magazine* in Adjuntas and kept producing events. In March 1992, The Cimarrón Theater Company mounted a production of *Valero and The Wheel of History* and, in October of the same year, performed *The Indigenous Zarzue-la of 1493*, both at the José Emilio Lugo High School.

A TEMPORARY VICTORY OVER MINING

In 1986, we held several conferences in opposition to mining at the University of Puerto Rico in Arecibo and in Río Piedras; in the communities of Castañer, Jayuya, Aibonito, and Carolina; at the Institute of Technology of Ponce; and at the Catholic University of Ponce and Arecibo. We participated in press conferences and radio programs. Newspapers kept reporting about Casa Pueblo's activities, and we welcomed visitors from different parts of the country. We held an anti-mining protest with 120 children from Guayanilla and created a support committee of twenty-two people in the San Juan metropolitan area. Our identity continued to evolve. Before, we were called "the mining people" and "the 2020 Plan people." Now, people were beginning to call us "the people from Casa Pueblo."

Some of our efforts were led by the Democratic Student Front, a group of young workshop members led by Ariel and Arturo. The organization was active in the local school, organized visits to the mining zone, distributed newsletters, and managed the Planting Hope project. One of their goals was to call attention to the problem of nuclear weapons, a matter that was being debated across the country. The Front had already participated in a 60-kilometer national march from Carolina to Ceiba against nuclear arms, and they also decided to organize an event in the plaza of Adjuntas on the subject. Before the event and under the direction of local graffiti artist Danny Torres, they painted a mural alluding to nuclear weapons. That night, Charles Hey Maestre from the Institute of Puerto Rican Civil Rights delivered an impactful speech, and Roy Brown, the internationally famous Puerto Rican singer-songwriter, gave a brilliant presentation.

Another memorable activity was *Latin American Encounters*, held in Casa Pueblo on August 16, 1986. Representatives from Argentina, Uruguay, Guatemala, Peru, Brazil, and Chile signed a document in support of our cause. Our local and national network now had an international network. Only ten days later, the headline story for the newspaper *El Mundo* reported the long-awaited victory. "A blow to exploitative mining on the island: celebrations as mining proposals are rejected. The Puerto Rican government will purchase 955 acres of land in the center of the island where the copper mines from the American Metal Climax Company (AMAX) were to be located: 750 acres in Utuado and Adjuntas, and the remaining 225 in Guayanilla."[1] Our arguments against Plan 2020 were now officially confirmed by others. The mining companies had indeed purchased 750 acres of land around the two main deposits; they had also purchased 225 acres at the port of Guayanilla to establish a refinery and a foundry. Just as we said, they had planned to construct an aqueduct running from the dam in Maragüez in Ponce to the port.

To be clear, our joy at this victory did not signal the end of our community effort. Often, groups fizzle out once they have reached their immediate goals. As we would soon learn, however, this would have been a tragic mistake, for it was not long before the specter of mining returned. We closed a glorious 1986 with two events, and the first was the Puerto Rico Religious Conference, meeting that year in Adjuntas. As a representative of the Arts and Culture Workshop, I was the featured speaker at the local Catholic Church. I gave testimony about the arduous anti-mining fight to an audience of more than 300 parishioners from across Puerto Rico. The second key event felt like a reward for our achievements: the rebuilding of the roof and the floors of Casa Pueblo. Arturo, Ariel, and two university students from Humacao, along with our friends Mingo Massol, Israel Plaza, and Enrique Linares, hammered and sawed with exemplary enthusiasm. A new chapter had begun for Casa Pueblo.

CHAPTER 6

IT'S DECIDED: WE SAY NO TO MINING!

800 students from the José Emilio Lugo High School in Adjuntas used their bodies to spell NO MINES as part of our third anti-mining campaign. May 10, 1995.

THE SPECTER OF MINING RETURNS

We began 1993 with our brothers and sisters in the diaspora by commemorating the birthday of our national hero, Eugenio María de Hostos. We designed an activity centered on Puerto Rican identity, calling it *We Are Boricuas* to honor our Indigenous roots. The Institute of Puerto Rican Culture and New York City Lore co-sponsored the event, which featured the musical groups Melodía Tropical, Trío Internacional, Los Pleneros de la 21, and Cuerdas de Borinquen. We presented the Arts and Culture Workshop's highest honor, the Eugenio María de Hostos Prize, to the illustrious musician from Adjuntas and resident of the Big Apple, Nerí Orta. From the countryside and from many towns, people came to pay homage with flowers, plaques, and gifts to this student of Ladislao Martínez Otero, a.k.a., El Maestro Ladí, historically the most influential composer and player of the Puerto Rican *cuatro,* the five-stringed instrument used to play traditional jíbaro music. The town square was full of life until one in the morning, affirming our group identity: Boricuas all, regardless of where we had been born or raised.

In February, we participated in a meeting of the coordinators of alternative economic projects, organized by our friend José Enrique Ayoroa Santaliz. We made a presentation about our Madre Isla Coffee and eco-tourism projects to an audience of nearly a hundred. Atilano Cordero Badillo, president of the Grande supermarket chain, made the promise, which he subsequently fulfilled, of collaborating with the Arts and Culture Workshop on our economic projects. We closed the month with a think-tank of students from the University of Puerto Rico at Casa Pueblo.

In March, we successfully completed multiple projects. One weekend, the distinguished Puerto Rican Sylvia Henríquez brought a group of twenty-seven teenagers from the Pro-Youth Association of Cucharillas in Cataño to visit the Finca Madre Isla Project for an intensive exchange with students from Adjuntas. It was an amazing learning opportunity for both groups, as was the visit by members of the Teacher's Association interested in learning about our model of community self-governance. During a week in April, twenty students from Roberto Clemente Community Academy in Chicago stayed in the cabins at the Finca Madre Isla. From this base camp, they went on day trips to various areas across Puerto Rico as part of a cultural immersion project. In May, we offered a workshop on the Puerto Rican tiple, the smallest of the three string instruments, which, along with the cuatro and the bordonua, compose the traditional orquesta jíbara (jíbaro orchestra). On March 28, the Julián Acosta Elementary School celebrated its Poetry Recital Festival at Casa Pueblo. As usual, week by week, and month by month, we processed and sold Madre Isla Coffee. Our community enterprise was now generating enough revenue to fund three part-time salaries, one student scholarship, and the cost of the physical maintenance of Casa Pueblo.

During the six years after our 1986 victory over mining interests, all our work was directed toward securing and strengthening the community's self-governance through national and cultural affirmation and through the development of alternative economic self-sufficiency via the Madre Isla Coffee Plantation and the Eco-Tourism project. But at the beginning of June, we received information from residents in the mining zone that companies were conducting new work in places known to have copper, gold, and silver deposits. After some research, we found out that these activities were related to scientific exploration in the area. We asked ourselves, "again?" Our country has always been preyed upon. When it wasn't coal plants, it was the radars in Vieques and Lajas, landfills, improper use of land to plant cement instead of crops, and the destruction of the environment. We had to go back and review all the information we had archived in the Hostos Library about the anti-mining fight between 1980 and 1986. Immediately, we protested through every means of communication, just like our stalwart brothers and sisters in Utuado had done to denounce new mine exploration on the outskirts of their town. On June 17, 1993, the Puerto Rico Department of Natural Resources was forced to clarify the situation. Within a week several mining companies publicly acknowledged that mining explorations were indeed under way, and one company took out an advertisement in several newspapers, including *El Vocero*, stating:

> Our company, Southern Gold Resources (USA) Inc., is currently evaluating the environmental aspects and the economic potential of the Cala Abajo deposits, under a permit granted by the Department of Natural and Environmental Resources.
>
> We have not yet concluded the study; it will take one and a half more years to complete. Nor have we requested a permit to begin mining these deposits.[1]

It was clear that mining explorations were underway, and there was no question about what we had to do. We understood that a new anti-mining fight had begun, and, as before, we were ready to do whatever was necessary to bring it to an end, this time for good. From that moment forward, all of our projects—Casa Pueblo, Madre Isla Coffee, and the Finca Madre Isla—would be managed with the goal of stopping the mines in perpetuity. The defense of our land and the resources that give life to this country would be integrated into all our cultural affirmation activities. The profits from selling coffee would be invested in the anti-mining campaign. This time we had more experience and three self-sustaining projects to rely on. We had become stronger as a community, and we knew we could stop the mines again.

A NEW STRATEGY: UNITY

We reconvened at Casa Pueblo to start redesigning our strategy in response to these new circumstances. We decided this time to focus on three main objectives, all in Adjuntas: creating opportunities for youth participation; developing new leadership; and incorporating other groups, such as religious, civic, and cultural organizations. We knew that if we succeeded in connecting with these sectors, it would strengthen the people's will to act on other matters affecting the community. We understood that change only came about through community unity, action, and hard work. We also thought it would be beneficial to create a wide opposition front, with Casa Pueblo as only one among many other organizations.

As a first step, we agreed to share our plan with the community, so that the people would know what was happening. On June 26, 1993, we participated in a radio program with Luis Francisco Ojeda in Ponce, and then on June 13 with WPJC Radio Gigante in Adjuntas. We also published our first report, *Work Starting at the Mining Zone 5KM from Adjuntas,* and distributed 3,000 copies of it in both rural and urban areas. As a sports commentator would later say, we turned the heat up. Based on our experience that successful community struggle cannot involve partisan attitudes, petty divisiveness, or elitism, we joined forces with the Utuado Pro-Environmental Foundation on July 11 and 14. Miguel Báez, Toño Rodríguez, and Capellita, among others, stood together as models of inter-organizational unity. We co-wrote and signed the document *For Our Life and for Puerto Rico* and when we finished, we said our goodbyes late that night, agreeing to continue working in our respective communities while still maintaining mutual communication and collaboration. This alliance would prove fundamental to our efforts.

After holding several smaller meetings, on August 5, 1993, we called a large assembly in Adjuntas. In good faith, we proposed that it would be best for the struggle if we created a large, united front of opposition. After two hours of discussion, the attendees turned down the proposal. In the end, we agreed that the coordination of the initiative would remain at Casa Pueblo. Proponents of this decision argued that, since we had been successful in the past, there was no reason to change our strategy. Under these circumstances, we resolved to boost participation in the fight. We reached out to new and old collaborators, like the university professor Lourdes Torres, Father José, surveyor Israel Plaza, members of the Pro-Environmental Committee of Tanamá, high school students, religious groups, and Ulises Torres, who had worked as an inspector in the US Bureau of Mines. With an expanded and diversified voice, we moved toward organizing a village forum.

A VILLAGE FORUM

We decided to celebrate our new strategy with a forum featuring a special guest, the Secretary of the Puerto Rico Department of Natural Resources. Several people expressed concerns, wondering why we would invite the principal proponent of the exploitative mining to Casa Pueblo. Some were sure that we had gone crazy. Nevertheless, we celebrated the Village Forum in Casa Pueblo on September 16, 1993, and the Secretary arrived on time, accompanied by an expert in mining geology and legal advisors. Tinti Deyá served as the moderator. Everything suggested that we were headed for a showdown, and indeed we were. It was a full house at Casa Pueblo, and the event was broadcast throughout the country via WPJC of Adjuntas, Radio Casa Pueblo, and WPAB of Ponce. We had ensured good attendance by sending out written invitations, making phone calls, and organizing the broadcast by WEUC-FM in Ponce. When the Secretary finished his presentation on the low environmental impact of what he called "small-scale" mining, others voiced their opposition to the mining proposal with a variety of arguments. We heard from anthropologist Ivor Hernández, of the Institute of Puerto Rican Culture; professor and poet Antonio Álvarez; agronomist María Eugenia Beck; Lilly Vélez, representing merchants; engineer Ulises Torres; Sister Gregoria of the Mercy Home for Girls; and fifteen university and high school students from Adjuntas. In the final part of the Village Forum, we organized a panel with Father José of the Catholic Church; Dr. Adalberto

Lugo Boneta; the agronomist and farmer Ariel Massol Deyá; Johanna Delgado, a junior at the José Emilio Lugo High School; and me. We put the visiting Secretary through an intense interrogation from people with different perspectives and specialties. The panel lasted an hour and a half.

We countered all his arguments in favor of mining with clear rebuttals. Each of the Secretary's main points—that the mining would be small-scale, that it amounted to only 10% of what was proposed in 1980, and that it would only exploit the Cala Abajo deposit—were refuted. The Secretary even conceded that, once the million-dollar investment of infrastructure was completed, mining would not stop at that 10%, affirming that once a deposit was exhausted, the companies would continue to look for others. On several occasions, he had to seek the advice of his team. It is worth noting that our panel of local representatives held various meetings before the forum to prepare ourselves to effectively ask our questions and counter the Secretary's responses. There was no room for improvisation, and in the panel, we successfully put all our technical, scientific, and social science expertise to work for the benefit of the Adjuntas communities. The then-mayor of Adjuntas, Rigoberto Ramos, who was among the participants, asked for the floor. After listening to both arguments, he said, he had changed his position and had decided to oppose the project. The president of the Municipal Assembly made the same announcement and promised to come up with a resolution. To those who were listening on the radio, saw the video that we showed, or read our news bulletin, it was clear that we could not accept this new exploitative mining proposal. The Village Forum was a powerful blow to mining interests at exactly the right time and place. We brought the opponent to the count of nine, and almost scored a knockout.

That day we realized that we could win again. We saw the potential of a unified community to transform a situation. We learned that we had to act with imagination and as a united front, expressing clear, forceful, and respectful arguments. We learned that we could create our own forums and that we did not have to depend on public hearings put on by the government where everything was fixed in advance. The Village Forum taught us to be protagonists and not just spectators. We also started to follow through on our promise to integrate local youth into our work and to open our spaces to other sectors of the community.

At the end of the Village Forum, we served Madre Isla coffee to all the guests, including those we considered to be our adversaries, but not our enemies. This was an important distinction to aid us in knowing where to aim our cannons. The unified voice of the people was beginning to have an impact. Other immediate results of the Village Forum included the *Assembly of the Cultural Centers of the Mountain Regions,* celebrated two weeks later at Casa Pueblo. There, the resolution *Por la Vida y Puerto Rico* (For Life and Puerto Rico) was written and approved by cultural centers in Utuado, Ángeles, Lares, Castañer, Jayuya, Barranquitas, Aibonito, and Adjuntas. The mayor of Adjuntas also signed the anti-mining resolution on behalf of the municipal assembly. As part of our overall strategy, we surveyed the teachers and students at the José Emilio Lugo High School in Adjuntas. The results revealed that 501 out of the 526 students, and 33 out of 36 teachers, also opposed mining. On October 27, we participated in another forum on mining at the Cultural Center of Utuado. The newspaper *Diálogo* interviewed us, and a professor of sociology at the University of Puerto Rico in Río Piedras brought her class to the event. The students pledged to support our fight through their studies and signed the anti-mining petition that was now circulating across Puerto Rico. Once again, the cycle of unity and solidarity grew from the center outward, and from the local to the national. However, there was still much to do and no time to rest on our laurels. We concluded 1993 in the spirit of the old saying: "There is no triumph without struggle, nor struggle without sacrifice."

DIVERSITY IN THE STRUGGLE

We started 1994 in much the same way as we did the previous year: commemorating the birth of Eugenio María de Hostos in the public plaza. This time, we awarded the Hostos Prize to a young improvisational singer-songwriter from Adjuntas, Edgardo Rivera Vega. Edgardo had started his career in the Arts and Culture Workshop as a child, singing about the defense of natural resources with the Puerto Rican traditional music group Mapeyé at one of their concerts in Adjuntas. Years earlier, in 1986, he had participated in the historic signing of the *Manifiesto de un pueblo que quiere vivir* (Manifesto of a People Who Want to Live), along with Andrés "El Jíbaro" Jiménez in Casa Pueblo. That night, which we called *Fiesta del Cafetal* (Coffee Plantation Festival), we presented him with the book *Trova borincana*, by Juan Manuel Delgado, and celebrated with the music of Café Colao. The event became very emotional when Neri Orta, master of the Puerto Rican cuatro who had received the Hostos Prize the year before, made a surprise appearance. Accompanied by other musicians from many areas of Puerto Rico, he came to pay homage to his successor.

Later that month we received a delegation of students from Columbia University and had a very rewarding conversation with them about the anti-mining struggle. In February 1994, we started offering sculpture classes under the direction of Francisco Pérez Cardona, an artist from Añasco who lived in San Francisco and had learned of Casa Pueblo through a serendipitous series of events. Ten years earlier, in 1984, Casa Pueblo had been touring the United States as part of our anti-mining campaign, visiting universities in eight states. At the University of San Francisco in California, we established a friendship with a man named Jimmy Emerman, who returned our visit in 1989. His interview of us was subsequently published with the title "The Environmental Struggle in Puerto Rico: Poison Paradise" in the *Earth Island Journal* of San Francisco. Pérez Cardona read the piece and became so enthusiastic about our work in Adjuntas that he reached out to us and offered his solidarity. Eventually, he attained a year-long sabbatical to do community volunteer work with us. His sculpture workshops were the product of another project from another time and another place, and this taught us is to keep putting energy into every interaction, even those that might seem insignificant.

Any relationship can someday bear unexpected fruit. It almost always takes time to see the results of our actions, and that is why we must be patient and persistent. Some people shy away from small interactions because they believe they will not lead to anything and are not worth the trouble. They forget that to build any tall structure, it is necessary to lay a foundation that may, in the end, be concealed. It was the accumulation of many smaller acts between 1980 and 1986 that led us to our first major victory against mining, and that would soon lead us to a second victory. We did not reach the summits of these mountains without first following an arduous and winding path to the top.

On February 21, we attended the wake of another unforgettable patriot who also accompanied us on many occasions: Oscar Collazo. Oscar was one of those who marched in 1985 through the streets of Adjuntas with a tree in hand as we sowed seeds of hope. He also helped produce the first golden beans of Madre Isla Coffee, to register books in the Hostos Library at Casa Pueblo, to reforest the Finca Madre Isla, and contributed to other important projects. Oscar lives on in our memory and in the important wisdom that he imparted to us.

March was a time of many different experiences. On March 1, Tinti and Alexis participated in a forum on mining at the University of Puerto Rico Mayagüez and made new alliances. Back in Adjuntas, we sponsored a conference at the José Emilio Lugo High School on the lyrical poetic form known as décima in the Caribbean and Latin America. We participated in radio programs at WPJC in Adjuntas and WEUC-FM in Ponce. As usual, we attended the bimonthly meeting of self-governing groups and economic design groups in San Germán. On March 19, we commemorated the birth of Puerto Rico's illustrious poet Julia de Burgos, though her birthday is actually on February 17. The distinguished group *Flor de Caña* came directly from Boston to perform their latest song in the public plaza of Adjuntas. Two younger members of the Workshop, Johanna and Ariel, were the speakers that night, explaining the concept of community self-governance. We sold coffee from our kiosk (we do not sell alcoholic beverages at our events), and we gave a demonstration on how to plant hydroponic lettuce greens. The demonstration was co-sponsored by the Monte Río Hotel, which also provided housing and food for the artists; the Ponce Bank; and the Panelli Hardware Store. Other supporters, like Paco Ramos, René Vera, Joe, and Mencho, also contributed. WPJC Radio Gigante broadcast the event in Adjuntas. It is crucial to note that the simultaneous efforts of a great many people resulted in significant communication and unity. There was no room for isolation or for people to be forgotten. Thus, little by little, we won over the town, while the mining company quietly continued to drill more exploratory boreholes in the rocks of our Boricua motherland.

ECOTOURISM AND MINING

A highlight for us at this time was the daylong symposium *Ecotourism in Puerto Rico: Realities and Projections,* held at the University of Puerto Rico on March 24th, 1994. It yielded terrific results. I was asked to speak on *Ecotourism Development Within a Community,* and I took the opportunity to unveil our Finca Madre Isla Project. The talk quickly summarized our fight against mining, focusing on our efforts to design an authentic ecotourism project in the mountains of Adjuntas. After the talk we met with people who were interested in alternative, pro-environmental economic designs and enthusiastic about our project. That month we also received a visit from two professors of ecology from the University of Michigan in Ann Arbor, who were familiar with our work because we had visited their university a decade earlier. On March 24, 25, and 26 we facilitated an exchange between high school students in Philadelphia and Adjuntas. The visiting students stayed at the Finca Madre Isla and became spokespeople for the anti-mining fight back in their home state of Pennsylvania.

On April 15th, we were invited to lead an event in Aguadilla to celebrate José de Diego's birthday and his contributions to the philosophy of self-governance, a topic dear to Casa Pueblo. José de Diego is commonly regarded as the father of the Puerto Rico independence movement in the nineteenth century, the poet whose firm NO against malicious attackers planted the seeds of the struggle for national liberation. "Among the poets," he once wrote, "I launch my rebellious verses, my cries of protest combatting the tyrants of our land, to the winds and the heart of the world." The invitation turned out to be very important for us. It focused our study on José de Diego and we discovered how close our thinking was to his. We felt that de Diego, like Corretjer, Rafael Cancel Miranda, Lolita Lebrón, and Carmín Pérez, lived within us, and we in them. Here was another dimension of unity and spiritual respect that both transcended time and humbly accompanied our group. On April 17, we presented the Camerata Coral in Concert, first at the San Joaquín School and then at the House of Mercy, both in Adjuntas. In addition to other activities, we offered a talk about sustainable agriculture at the Adjuntas High School, and I read children's stories at the Yahuecas School. For a week, students from the Roberto Clemente High School in Chicago returned to the Finca Madre Isla, joyful to be back again on their land.

On May 3, 1994, representatives of Southern Gold Resources came to Adjuntas. First, they went to visit the mayor intending to convince him that the mining project would confer many benefits and to get his approval. Then, they arrived unexpectedly at Casa Pueblo soliciting a meeting with me, to which I agreed. When I asked the purpose of the visit, they explained that the mayor had told them to talk to Casa Pueblo first, and, if they convinced us, to return to see him. Our response, of course, was a resounding NO, imbued with the same spirit that drove José de Diego's resistance to the colonial powers in his day. The experience speaks for itself: our social power had deeply penetrated and transformed the town's political power structure. Late May and early June of 1994 brought another significant milestone for the anti-mining struggle. More than two hundred representatives from South, Central, and North America, Asia, Europe, and Puerto Rico, attended the *World Tourism Congress for the Environment* in San Juan. At this international summit, we shared our perspective on eco-tourism, explaining that successful eco-tourism must be sensitive to the environment and to the country. It should be the type of tourism that respects the trees, birds, and endangered species, and it must also respect the people and culture of Puerto Rico, both of which are today threatened with extinction by exploitative mining. One of the field seminars of the Congress took place in Casa Pueblo. During the meeting, we approved a resolution opposing exploitative mining and supporting eco-tourism as an economically viable alternative that was compatible with the environment and eliminated mining. The resolution was later presented and approved during the plenary session of the Congress at the Condado Hotel Plaza, with the governor of Puerto Rico and the Secretary of the Department of Natural and Environmental Resources in attendance. This time, we refuted mining with concrete and viable alternatives. Unfortunately, our victory did not come with the support from the United Nations Special Committee on Decolonization, or C-24, an assembly sometimes marked by diplomatic hypocrisy. Instead, it came about thanks to our ongoing work of building a self-governing community.

Extending our influence from the local to the national and then to the global levels yielded positive outcomes for our self-governing community and became a new formula in our work. A week later, we inaugurated a sculpture exhibit titled "Recovering What Was Once Lost in Casa Pueblo." The sculptor Francisco Pérez Cardona returned from San Francisco on another sabbatical and unveiled his bust of the workshop activist Osvaldo Rodríguez Blondet, in a small park that now carries his name. In a virtuoso performance, clarinet master Ricardo Velázquez elevated the ceremony to the level of sublime inspiration. In October 1994, we held a ceremony to harvest our first coffee crop at the Finca Madre Isla, with more than thirty children and as many adults. The ceremony started when we all dropped, in unison, the first beans we had gathered into large tin cans. The sound reverberated like drums of war and of peace. In two and a half hours, we had collected close to 10 bushels of coffee beans. That night in Casa Pueblo, the children dramatized the work they had done during the day and the Gira Criolla Group, along with improvisational folk singers Edgardo Rivera and Julio César Sanabria, affirmed our identity and desires through their exquisite music and singing.

A STING OPERATION AND THE COMMUNITY'S RESPONSE

Until this point, all our work had continued at a steady pace to prepare us for an open confrontation with the mining interests. The companies had already finished their tests and were preparing to present their mining proposals. Then, we received a low blow that knocked the wind out of us for a few days. On October 16, 1994, and in the same location where we had celebrated our first coffee harvest a few weeks before, over a hundred FBI agents came looking for Puerto Rican independence activist and militant Filiberto Ojeda Ríos. It turned out that when my mother died, he called the funeral home to express his condolences from Hartford, Connecticut, where he was under house arrest. Furthermore, he had visited us wearing an ankle monitor to learn about our project. One of his visits coincided with an event in the plaza. He stayed on the sidelines until someone identified him and people began to approach him to talk, embrace him, and take pictures. He later removed his ankle monitor and went underground. Sometime after that, the front page of *The San Juan Star* reported having spotted Filiberto on the streets of Adjuntas distributing Madre Isla Coffee. When national hero Oscar Collazo heard about it, he wrote to ask if he also qualified to distribute Madre Isla Coffee. The show of force that came down upon us included helicopters, planes, dogs, and boats. It was a massive operation. Heavily armed, they detained many people on the street with no explanation. Some were hand-cuffed, others were made to lie face down on the road, and still others were pulled out of their cars, cited, and detained. The FBI also harassed the fishermen in Garzas Lake, which borders our plan-tation, and entered a local factory, thinking that Filiberto might be working there. With guns in hand, they marched through our town and neighborhoods, putting up signs on light posts, trees, and stores, offering a reward to anyone who would help find the wanted man. In their search at the Finca Madre Isla, they found a tall flagpole with the single-starred flag aloft and free. They also found the footprints of children, men, and women; of musicians, poets, and workshop members, all Boricuas who were searching for the path to a "future without fail," as the poet Juan Antonio Corretjer taught us. Two weeks later, they would also face a com-munity's response.

Groups regularly confront the issue of community con-flict mediation. When conflicts develop, it is important not to lose sight of the main objectives of the group, nor should one improvise by addressing individual issues as they arise. Instead, one should conduct careful analysis of the situation and seek suitable responses. In the community response to the FBI operation,practiced the three central principles of com-munity development according to sociologist Alain Touraine:

The Identity Principle: We kept focused on what we were doing and indentified us—the fight against mining.

The Opposition Principle: We defined the opposition as the government and the companies advocating for the mining operations, not the FBI.

The Totality Principle: We never lost sight of the big picture or our ultimate goal, which was to stop the mining.

We deduced that the barbaric FBI sting operation was, among other things, intended to divert us from our core mission and isolate us from the community by using fear tactics at the precise moment the mining companies were readying their proposal for exploitation.

Realizing how dire the situation was, we lost no time in stopping these new attempts to destroy Puerto Rico's lands and territory. To go back into isolation would be the path to community failure. We needed to respond to the operation immediately. We decided to use the tool that we always carried with us: Puerto Rican culture. In less than two weeks, we organized a Community Festival at the Finca Madre Isla. First, we visited neighbors and friends to secure their commitment to participate and contribute to the activity on October 30. We also invited artists to join us: Trío Río Mar, Jaime Reyes, Gregorio Rivera, Edgardo Rivera, Tato Ramos, Zualbi, Iván and Aniel Irizarry (from Adjuntas), and Mapeyé with Rolando Silva. When we visited neighbors to invite them to the festival and inform them that Filiberto was not at the Finca Madre Isla, they frequently interrupted us to say that protecting him and having him there would be the right thing for us to do. They mentioned that, had they known about his presence, they would have offered him food and lodging themselves. Most people were in favor of protecting a person who they believed hadn't hurt anybody. It was an unforgettable experience and a testament to our fierce community solidarity. Between the sun and the rain, falling like petals from the sky, the festival began with some 500 people in attendance. Among the national supporters were members of the Cultural Centers of Jayuya, Utuado, Vega Alta, Manatí, Casa Corretjer, the Pro-Environment Foundation of Utuado, and friends from San Juan, Ponce, Guayama, Aguada, and San Sebastián. Of all the people from the neighborhood that we invited, ninety-six percent came to the event and many brought food and refreshments. Two percent excused themselves, and the other two percent had joined the party of the fearful. Doubts were dissipated. The community responded resoundingly to the aggression and all feelings of helplessness and isolation dissolved.

United in songs of rebellion, we took a deep breath that night and reaffirmed our faith in the community and our stance against mining. We spent November and December 1994 reevaluating what to do and how to do it. Through this process, a new organizational strategy came about. We decided to expand Casa Pueblo's board of directors. We chose twenty candidates and divided the task of approaching them with our invitation. We thought that it was possible that the FBI operation would negatively affect their decision to join the leadership body. However, the next week when we met to share the results, we found that of the seventeen people we invited, sixteen said that it would be an honor for them to join Casa Pueblo's board of directors. And, oh, what great a joy it was to feel so supported by our community! The reorganized structure made us stronger and put us in a better situation to go back on the offensive. With a larger and revitalized board in place, we bid farewell to 1994 and left the FBI operation behind us. We launched into 1995 with faith, hope, and our eyes set on victory for the community.

A NEW ALTERNATIVE PROJECT

Our participation in various forums on eco-tourism throughout 1994 allowed us to get to know several distinguished people with exceptional personal qualities. Among them were Edgardo González, Ivelisse Gorbea, Fernando Silva, Vicente Quevedo, Carmen Pérez, Digna Delgado, Judith Amador, and others who had joined us before at Casa Pueblo. With their help, a plan was born for improving a project already underway: interpretive guides for ecological and cultural tourism. We inaugurated the new project in 1995 by training young people to identify and teach about the flora, fauna, and socio-cultural aspects of Adjuntas. We received forty applications for fifteen positions. Training took place at the Finca Madre Isla. We started to build an inventory of birds, native trees, and endangered species of trees, and we created self-guided trails for visitors to walk on and learn about the local ecosystem. The eco-tourism project was evolving at the Finca Madre Isla and would eventually become a self-sufficient source of revenue and jobs. We conducted similar work at nearby areas of interest, like the Guilarte Forest, the Garzas Lake, rivers, ponds, and historic places in the neighborhood. The experience enriched our concept of what an ecotourism community project could be, and it now included the element of sensitivity towards nature, history, and culture. Some people who had participated in the early days of the anti-mining struggle became guides, thus bringing our struggle full circle. In this period of working with the fifteen youths and field technicians, we learned that the mining deposits were below an important life-sustaining ecosystem: the humid, subtropical forest. The forest, with the crystal-clear waters of the Pellejas and Viví Rivers, an annual rainfall of one hundred inches, and a particular range of temperatures, has important ecological functions. It controls sedimentation and erosion and supports a healthy flora and fauna. Preserving this vigorous, biodiverse ecosystem, would become a major argument for eliminating mining. Our data supported an alternative proposition: turn the mining zone into a forest of the Puerto Rican people, a People's Forest. But to make this idea a reality and a legacy to the island and global humanity, we would first have to vanquish the mining project.

ONWARD TO VICTORY

On February 17, we celebrated the third anti-mining rally with an all-day program that featured a concert by the international group Sol y Canto who played for a bustling crowd in the plaza. We also enjoyed the performances of other musicians, poetry readings by local authors, and artisanal exhibitions. TV Channel 6 devoted an episode of their program *Desde Mi Pueblo* (From My Hometown) to the event, including a demonstration of our hydroponic lettuce cultivation system designed by Ariel Massol Deyá. On May 24, our neighbors at the Pro-Environment Foundation in Utuado held a grand municipal assembly formally closing the door to mining Utuado. The Finca Madre Isla continued to be the star of the moment. Students from the Roberto Clemente School in Chicago, young people from Philadelphia, a community from the Cu-cha-ri-llas de Cataño neighborhood, and twenty-seven U.S. students from sixteen different states came to visit us and stayed at the plantation. We also trained our young guides to give talks about mining at their schools. Sharing our stories through print media, radio, and television was part of a strategy to reach all of Puerto Rico. We participated in radio programs on WEUC-FM, WPAB, WKAQ with Luis Francisco Ojeda, Noti Uno, Radio Raíces of San Sebastián, and WPJC of Adjuntas. We were featured on the TV program *Ocurrió así* (That's How It Happened), and, through CNN, news of our struggle spread to the rest of Latin America and the continental United States. These media platforms, along with Obed Cintron's program *Hacia el 2000* (Toward 2000) and the articles published in the high school's *Revista Escolar* (Student Newspaper), were crucial in winning over the Puerto Rican people to our side in the struggle.

Shifting our thinking from the local to the national level, we carried out three decisive actions in May and June 1995:

- A press conference "from the sky." In a meeting between workshop faculty and the young guides, we agreed that saying a lot with few words would be most powerful.

After debating various ideas, Inés thought of having high school students spell out a message with their bodies. Tinti led the operation. Almost all the teachers embraced the idea and made it happen. Rosa Delia Meléndez of Channel 4 and other journalists attended the press conference, which consisted of eight hundred students in the parking lot of the José Emilio Lugo High School, forming the words NO MINAS ("NO MINES"). The image was captured from a helicopter and broadcast on television for all of Puerto Rico to see. The interviews with the students were also impressive, and this symbol of unity, strength and the will to overcome had a great national impact.

- *NO A LA EXPLOTACIÓN MINERA* (NO TO MINING) was the front page news story of *El Nuevo Día* on May 28, 1995. The report covered four full pages and highlighted Casa Pueblo's role in the struggle.
- On June 10, 1995, Casa Pueblo called for a march to the Cala Abajo deposit, with the slogan *We Already Decided: NO MINING.* Children, teenagers, adults, and businesspeople from Adjuntas participated in this historical act, alongside members of the national anti-mining movement. Together, we planted trees to express our intent to transform the mining zone into a forest for the Puerto Rican people and hoisted the Puerto Rican flag on land that we proclaimed to be free of mining.

These three events marked the end of the anti-mining struggle. Two weeks later, open-pit mining was prohibited by law. Some said it was a pyrrhic victory because legislators could change the law again at any moment. However, as Ariel Massol Deyá put it, "The truth is that the Puerto Rican people wrote their own law from the streets, ruled out mining, and saved Puerto Rico from an ecological catastrophe. And if the mining companies come back and try again, they know that we will return and write the law again, like we just did."

LOOKING BACK ON OUR ANTI-MINING CAMPAIGN

The anti-mining campaign marked the first fifteen years of Casa Pueblo, from 1980 to 1995. The following are some of the highlights of what was, and continues to be, a learning process. They stand out as worthy of reflection and analysis and provide lessons on how to confront Puerto Rico's colonial reality:

- The first anti-mining rally, which only one person attended, was an act of faith. We understand that faith is not just hope, but also, an action that goes along with a promise of love and justice. This first failure taught us an important lesson: one must design effective fighting strategies. Improvising is an unacceptable error.
- To activate the community, we planned the concert *The Motherland Within* around areas of particular interest to different people. This way, everyone could participate in accordance with their personal motivating factors and, regardless of the size of their contribution, take part in a process of participatory democratization. It was an inclusive experience; what was exclusive was left behind. We discarded the kind of individualistic protagonism that marginalized individuals and social sectors.
- Science became an educational tool and its study a constant practice whenever seeking answers and reliable explanations to help the community make informed decisions.
- The process taught us that science alone cannot further the cause; culture also needs to be incorporated as an instrument of identity, belonging, and action. The participation of a community with both knowledge and cul-

tural pride yielded positive results. *Territory* and *culture*, especially useful in a colonized country, became essential concepts in our fight.

- From this interpretation and practice emerged our work equation: *science + culture + community = change and victories*. The social-community economy was an important outcome of this formula.
- One of our first challenges as a group was to learn for ourselves about mining so that we would not have to depend on outside experts; this does not mean we should isolate ourselves.
- From within, we developed a new concept: *voz propia*, a voice of one's own. The result of having a firm and independent position led us to this clear idea: "Republic or colony, zero mines in Puerto Rico."
- Another key lesson emerged from *voz propia*: do not enter into alliances with politicians or political parties. Such alliances weaken community self-governance and stunt its growth.
- Applying the principles of *identity*, *opposition*, and *totality*, which proved to be essential for strengthening governance, avoids errors and clarifies strategies.
- We proved that defense of the territory is a necessary condition for guaranteeing the development of self-sustaining communities.
- The nascent projects of self-sustaining development helped to establish a new community paradigm of growth and stability.
- Combining *voz propia* with independent strategies moves community self-governance along a path of action "from the bottom up, and toward social-political change."

I will close this summary of our first stage by stating the obvious: had mining started, we would not be here to chronicle the origins of Casa Pueblo. Because of this, I would like to add a community perspective on the current global problem of neoextractivism, which has been adopted by both progressive and conservative governments as official state policy. Neoextractivism is causing unprecedented ecological and social catastrophes, such as the loss of our forests, including the lungs of our planet in the Amazon Basin. It is also degrading our bodies of water, including glaciers, and contributing to the loss of biodiversity, including long-established human communities. The following are some news summaries that point to the gravity of the problem.

- "Over 6,000 proposals for exploitative mining in protected areas of the Amazon." The report says that the amount of fossil fuel extraction in the most extensive rainforest in the world is "alarming," with more than 800 permits already approved for mining in protected areas. "To add to this," according to the World Wildlife Federation, "there are currently more than 6,800 proposals under review, and although it is possible that the majority of these will not be approved, the numbers demonstrate the magnitude of the threat to this area."[2]
- "Large-scale mining threatens snow-capped Mount Pastoruri in Peru," September 2, 2016. The glaciers of Mt. Pastoruri in Peru have lost between 60 and 65% of their perennial snow, as a consequence of global warming and the large-scale mining that is practiced in this area.[3]
- "The Minerales de Occidente company is making entire communities in Copán disappear. They have caused three communities to disappear already, and they are now threatening to disappear our dead too because they want to extract gold from the cemetery," Honduran environmentalist Genaro Rodríguez from La Unión, Copán, said in the Popular Forum on Progress Radio on July 29, 2016.[4]
- "Director of the World Bank justifies the assassination

of Berta Cáceres," May 1, 2016. During the Theological Seminar of the Union in New York, the president of the World Bank, Jim Yong Kim, called the assassination of

the Indigenous leader Berta Cáceres an "incident": "You cannot do the type of work that we are trying to do and not have some incidents like this."[5]

PART II

A TERRITORIAL APPROACH
TO WATER AND FORESTS

CHAPTER 7

MOVING FROM PROTEST
TO PROPOSITIONS

During the celebrations of the centenary of the Puerto Rican
flag and our victory over mining in the town plaza, and with the
approval of some 10,000 people, we agreed to evolve 'from protest to propositions', from fighting mines to protecting forests.
December 22, 1995.

FROM MINES TO FORESTS

At first, our territorial approach arose from the confrontation over the mining proposals that would have caused an ecological catastrophe. This struggle introduced us to a beautiful process of socially and culturally constructing our sense of identity as intimately connected to the territory. Our territory was transformed into a national patrimony through our struggle. Casa Pueblo celebrated its coming of age on December 22, 1995. Only one person attended the first anti-mining conference in 1980, but this time 10,000 people crowded the plaza in Adjuntas.

They came to celebrate three things:

- *Victory over the mining companies.* That night, we celebrated our triumph over indifference, apathy, and negligence after a struggle lasting over fifteen years. We had saved the watershed. From the town of Adjuntas to San Juan and the south and west of the country, we successfully stopped the destruction of our water resources at the hands of mining companies, and ensured the potable water supply for millions of our fellow countrymen. This was water for the economy and water for life. Almost 37,000 acres of land had been saved because of the struggle, which spanned the local and international levels.
- *The Centennial of the Puerto Rican Flag.* We paid homage to our Boricua nationality by honoring the centennial of the Puerto Rican flag. We gave away thousands of flags to local residents, the same flag that in the past had been criminalized. For the first time, the one-star flag flew over Casa Pueblo. Thousands participated and sang the Puerto Rican national anthem with sublime emotion, becoming the protagonists of that historic moment.
- *Moving from protest to propositions.* Casa Pueblo turned the celebration into a town hall meeting to shift the discourse from just protesting mining to initiating a

positive proposal for the future. At the same time, we did not wish to diminish the importance of protest, which had brought us to this point. We therefore proposed transforming the mining zone into a People's Forest. We left behind the slogan "No to Mining" (*No a las Minas*) in favor of the enthusiastic proclamation "Yes to the Forest" (*Bosque sí*).

The *Yes to the Forest* campaign began a month later. New volunteers and collaborators joined to form a new front in the struggle. They created newsletters, conducted workshops, and held meetings in the neighborhoods of Adjuntas. To better understand the issue, the campaign consulted national specialists in ecology and biology and held a forum called *The Importance of the Tropical Forest*. A new journey of action and learning began.

AN ASSEMBLY OF BOYS AND GIRLS

The local campaign continued to grow in scale. Sixth grade students from the Washington Irving Elementary School in Adjuntas participated in workshops on the importance of forests. Seven months later, Casa Pueblo held an "Assembly of Boys and Girls" in celebration. The resolution announcing the Assembly read:

> We, the boys and girls of Adjuntas and Puerto Rico, meeting in Assembly today, August 10, 1996 in Casa Pueblo, by virtue of the law that confers upon us the right to life and guarantees the lives of the generations to come, and as our legacy for Puerto Rico and humanity, declare: First: That this Forest, saved by the will of so many sons and daughters of Puerto Rico over the past 35 years, shall be known as the Bosque del Pueblo, the People's Forest. [. . .]

METAMORPHOSIS OF A SPACE: THE PEOPLE'S FOREST

Four months after the Assembly of Boys and Girls, both community and forestry history were made in Puerto Rico with the formal designation of *Bosque del Pueblo*, The People's Forest. It was the first forest reserve to be established through community initiative in Puerto Rico, and the first to be managed by a self-governing organization, thanks to a groundbreaking agreement with the Department of Natural and Environmental Resources (DRNA), the government agency that up until then had held the monopoly in managing Puerto Rico's forests. Fifty years had passed since the last forest reserve had been designated by the government. Adding another reserve through our community initiative changed public policy around forestry and added to our national community agenda.

It also marked a larger shift. At the time, the importance of forests, ecology, environmental protection, sustainable development, and community forest management were not priorities for the country. Establishing the People's Forest brought these issues to the forefront and gave them new visibility. The People's Forest became the center of a territorial approach no longer focused primarily on opposing mining, but on promoting local, sustainable, and self-sustaining development. Again, this idea was generated at the local level and rose to the national level.

COMMUNITY MANAGEMENT

We celebrated the signing of the co-management agreement for the People's Forest and the inauguration of the Community Management Council on December 7, 1996, in the Adjuntas public plaza. Attendance was high. Edgardo González, director of the Division of Land Management, signed the agreement on behalf of the Department of Natural and Environmental Resources (DRNA), and I signed for Casa Pueblo. We called the event *Adjuntas and Latin America Celebrate the Community Management of the People's*

Forest. Folk singers from Argentina, Uruguay, and Chile sang for us, as did the Traditional Mapeyé Ensemble of Puerto Rico. We were moved listening to José Curbelo, Roberto Airala, Rodolfo Lemble, Marchesini, Tito Fernández, and the Temucano improvise, "No to the mines / I sing for Casa Pueblo / for Adjuntas, the Sleeping Giant / and the Bosque del Pueblo." The Rafael Aparicio Jiménez Middle School theater group and the environmental club from Washington Irving Elementary School in Adjuntas also participated. We received good press coverage, too. *El Nuevo Día* published an article titled "Casa Pueblo to co-manage the Forest in Adjuntas," and the title of an editorial in *El Vocero* read, "Agreement in Adjuntas to Co-manage the Forest." Once again, we had effectively used our tested formula of *science + culture + community = change and victories*, this time applying it to the creation of Puerto Rico's first community forest. We had begun to evolve, from protest to propositions. A new chapter for Casa Pueblo had begun.

A NEW CHAPTER WITH MANY NEW FACES

After passing through our trial by fire and putting a stop to mining on our lands, Casa Pueblo began a new chapter, with new actors and new ideas. Patriotic, committed, and humble, new volunteers joined our work alongside experts from many disciplines and veterans of the movement. Hand in hand, we marched together towards an alternative model of local community development from the bottom up. Many of these new volunteers were young people and others were specialists in fields as diverse as forestry, biology, biogeography, music, radio, engineering, social sciences, agriculture, and law. The partnership also included universities, professors, students, and administrative staff. They joined an exceptional team that carried out indispensable day-to-day duties with devotion. The organization grew with miraculous speed, keeping up with our evolving mission. We created task forces corresponding to the major needs of the mission and capabilities of the volunteers.

We had a Board of Community Management, a Scientific-Cultural Technical Commission, and a Volunteer Corps, as well as groups that focused on legal and economic matters. Physical labor was a vital part of our work too, and the Boricua field workers–the archetypical *macheteros* adept with the hammer, the pick, and the shovel–worked proudly to build and maintain our infrastructure, ensuring that our projects could continue. Our work opened the door for other communities to consider alternative ways to empower themselves by leveraging their natural resources. We started sharing our concept of *community management* and our awareness of the island as a shared geographical patrimony with other communities. Out of this process, three concepts emerged that helped us to better understand our relationship to the land and our role in it: coevolution, topophilia, and social territory.

Coevolution

Given everything we had accomplished, we asked ourselves if real emancipation and social transformation was a viable goal. What would we need to maintain community cohesion permanently? We concluded that for community self-governance to last, rather than fade away once the original goals that gave rise to it are achieved, the goals and the approach to achieving them must continuously evolve. Lasting community self-governance requires reciprocal changes: the evolution of the self along with the evolution of the work. Unless the self itself evolves, the work of community self-governance cannot evolve. This is mutual coevolution in which both parts interact, reinforce each other, and grow together. We evolve to orchestrate social change and attend to vital everyday concerns like education, health, poetry, and art. We also evolve to form a new human being, one that becomes socially committed and loving, through daily practices. Without both types of evolution, community self-governance simply disappears. Extensive democratic participation and volunteerism were foundational to permanent cohesion.

Topophilia

When I was a child, the forests, the mountains, and the rivers were my constant source of inspiration and my challenges in countless adventures. To walk, explore, camp, bathe in the river, and discover the flora and fauna of Adjuntas shaped my identity and happiness. These recollections and later developments told me that something was still missing in our theory. I found that missing piece in the concept of topophilia.

For the Chinese-American human geographer Yi-Fu Tuan, topophilia is a feeling of "attachment" that unites human beings and the places with which they identify. The field of geography defines this concept as "an affective bond between a people and a place or environmental setting." It speaks of a shared place, a constructed territory. The French philosopher Gaston Bachelard used the term *topophilia* for the first time in his book, *The Poetics of Space*. He writes that topophilia aspires to "determine the human value of the sorts of space that may be grasped, that may be defended against adverse forces, the space that we love."[1] Etymologically, the term comes from two words: *topos* (place) and *philia* (love of). Simply put, *topophilia* is the love of place and landscape.

Topophilia is also one of the concepts that postmodernist geography uses to reevaluate the concepts of *landscape, territory,* and *place*, to explain the relationship between human beings and their environment, and to reevaluate what we mean by ecology, environment, and the fight to preserve it. "Thus," writes Zerecero Cisneros Braulio in "The Concept of Topophilia in Geography: A New Form of Explaining the Appropriation of Spaces by Subjec*t*," "topophilia appears as a concept that explains how human beings appropriate their spaces, of how they take root or not, depending in the most profound way on their manners of being and thinking."[2] Francisco

Garrido Peña adds: "We understand topophilia to be a biocultural instrument for the adaptation of our species. The aesthetic and moral emotions that landscapes cause in us are very useful for the construction of a moral and ecological economy."[3] By embracing the concept of topophilia, self-governing communities can better understand their deep connection to place. This is important in the context of accelerating environmental degradation, the globalization of finance, and growing social inequality. Topophilia is at the heart of Casa Pueblo's commitments and practices. It is born from the defense of a territory threatened by mining, and from the commitment to manage the People's Forest, which has become our sacred place, a landmark of what we consider to be a social territory.

Social Territory

I always thought that Adjuntas belonged to me and to all who lived there. The plaza, the school, the playground, the church, and the forests all gave life meaning. None of it was private property, but rather a commons. For this reason, we took care of it, we enjoyed it, and we missed it when we were away. We identified both with Adjuntas and with Puerto Rico. The small place, and the larger country. The local and the national. My own experience of identifying with Adjuntas in this way clarified the concept of *social territory* for me. The concept of social territory comes from the social sciences; it refers to a geographically defined space that a group of people collectively understand or around which they build a sense of community. The social territory, defined as such, is real to the degree that people collectively understand it. As common understanding of a social territory grows, so too does the territory itself. This shared sense of place can be achieved both through activism and through the activities of daily life that bind people to place.

Social territories are constantly being constructed and reconstructed through the participatory practices that define community self-governance. They are made real through shared struggles, which build a sense of identity. The social territory is where knowledge is produced, and where social, economic, and cultural values form and reform. The social territory is a stage for resistance and opposition to projects that can adversely impact it. It is also a place where utopian dreams are born. Community self-governance is an engine of social change and is often built through social territory. We can find examples in Indigenous and Black organizations with deep ties to land and ancestry and in farming and environmental organizations whose work is intimately tied to the land. The concept of territory is not limited to geography and physical space, but also has social, cultural, environmental, economic, and organizational dimensions. The social territory is born from this feeling of attachment, of topophilia. In the words of Bachelard, it aspires to "determine the human value of the sorts of space that may be grasped, that may be defended against adverse forces, the space that we love."[4]

OUR SOCIAL TERRITORY GROWS

For Casa Pueblo, the process of community planning and the concurrent struggles against mining could be considered the first phase of establishing a social territory. An early milestone was the acquisition of an old house at 30 Rodolfo González Street in Adjuntas. In 1985, the building became an independent cultural center and our headquarters. This set in motion the process of building a shared identity with a strong attachment to place. With roots now established, our social territory grew. In 1986 we began the project *Sembrando Esperanzas* (Sowing Hope) and in 1991 we began an ecological tourism project, the Finca Madre Isla. Throughout this period, the social territory continued to take shape during the struggle, led by the community of the Tanamá neighborhood, to stop the municipal government of Adjuntas from constructing a landfill at the headwaters of the Tanamá River, a fight we won in

1989. Similarly, our concept of *social territory* incorporated the liberation struggle in solidarity with the community of Vacas Saltillo, when in 1996 we successfully halted the construction of 103 residences with septic tanks on the shores of Lake Garzas in Adjuntas, a project that had already been approved by the Puerto Rico Planning Board. I remember the Feliciano Family, Mirito, Afortunado, and his wife and family, Sonia Maldonado, and others, who made the brave decision to carry out civil disobedience to save the waters that feed the municipalities of Peñuelas and Ponce. This saved Lake Garzas, considered to have the best water quality in all of Puerto Rico. As a result, the lake became part of a shared social territory.

THE PEOPLE'S FOREST AND LA OLIMPIA FOREST

Our practice of social territory was further solidified at the end of 1996 when we converted 36,000 acres of land that had been allocated for mining into a People's Forest managed by the community. This was another victory at the local level that had national implications. The governance and administration of the People's Forest have been carried out by an extraordinary group of volunteers, specialists, academics, and communities for more than two decades. Science and culture worked as one in the People's Forest, offering a new paradigm of forest management by and for Puerto Rican communities. The formal designation of the forest and the creation of the community management regime transformed the space into a social territory run by the people. It gave credence to alternative ways of life, asserting that the people have social, economic, political, cultural, and environmental rights. We consolidated this reclaimed land into a social habitat that we held in common, that was participatory, and that people understood experientially. We became attached to this landscape and are leaving our historical footprint on it.

Our attachment became evident in the face of the catastrophic fire that burned almost 100 acres of land in March of 2014. This disaster caused the emergency activation of the Council of Community Management of the People's Forest which, in coordination with other regions of the country, planned and carried out the ecological recovery of our emblematic social territory. At the event *El Bosque del Pueblo Reverdece* (Bosque del Pueblo Becomes Green Again) on the 26th of April of 2014, we planted more than one thousand trees with the help of people from all corners of Puerto Rico. We worked to the sound of music, chanting "this forest is mine!" to reinforce our cultural attachment to the forest. This experience was repeated in 2017, on the fifteenth anniversary of the Julián Chiví Festival, which celebrates the annual migratory return of our endangered black-whiskered bird friend from South America to the island. We celebrated with university courses, reforestation, camping, and cultural events, as well as other activities.

The concept of *social territory* has echoed throughout Puerto Rico and continues to be important in the broader movement for social change. We see social territories develop around other reclaimed spaces throughout Puerto Rico, at our beaches, agricultural areas, natural reserves, and plazas, all evidence of communities joining to defend these places against harmful projects that the government and large companies try to implement. The Olimpia Forest was another such initiative that further expanded our social territory. For several years, Casa Pueblo had been petitioning the government to designate 437 acres of forest in Adjuntas as protected land, and in 2004, we signed a community management agreement with the Department of Natural Resources, similar to the contract for Bosque del Pueblo. The principal argument for the designation was the importance of the forest as a hydrological resource: it protects the headwaters of the Río Grande de Arecibo, which supplies potable water to more than 1.5 million people from Adjuntas to San Juan. Our territorial focus soon expanded to the national level with several new initiatives, including the Bosque Modelo (Model Forest) in Utuado, the Fund for the Acquisition and Conservation of Lands in Puerto Rico, the Conservation Plan for Adjuntas and Adjacent Plans, and the establishment of new protected areas.

REVALORIZING THE GEOGRAPHIC COUNTRY

Many people lack an identity that relates to their national territory, their geographic space, and their landscape because our education system does not relate people to their land. The concept of social territory becomes even more important in this context: it re-affirms, protects, and collectivizes the process of identity formation, giving people a sense of belonging. With the expansion of the social territory, Casa Pueblo sowed seeds that would shape our future and change the way that other groups and even the government worked. The new natural reserves, the forests, and the new community managers played an important role in these changes. A program of tours and visits to Casa Pueblo and the surrounding forests became a key component of a broader strategy to scale up our efforts, and soon we were hosting between 2,500 and 3,000 visitors every month. The team of field guides and staff carried out the daily operations of these programs and provided thorough explanations and technically rigorous education to our visitors.

The lectures and tours contributed in turn to the evolution of the social territory in several ways:

- They *reconnected* the people with their forest and their national territory, fostering a sense of identity and a consciousness of being part of the Puerto Rican nation.
- They *revalorized* the forests and the landscape by acknowledging them as spaces of knowledge production and transformative education; they quantified and recognized ecological resources like clean air and clean water as values.
- They *promoted* the recuperation of the common good, which included the visitor's commitment to the land.

- They *recovered the idea and practice* of a common good. In other words, community members began to assume responsibilities that they previously considered to be the exclusive domain of government.
- They *revalued* the forest by expanding its purpose and reach through a Forest School that functioned as a pedagogical space to hold field workshops for public and private school students in the region, in addition to hosting guided visits, research, and cultural activities.

These initiatives were much more than ecological conservation, economic development, or community autonomy projects. They helped to build an idea of a nation that is built from community self-governance, that begins at the local scale and grows out to the national level, as we will see in later chapters. In Puerto Rico, the idea and practice of social territory represents a sustained response to colonialism. The idea of social territory refutes the imperial ownership of the Island, declaring itself a territory in its own right and distinct from the United States. The community practice of social territory says: "This territory is my country and it belongs to you and to everyone who loves and defends it." The idea and practice of social territory seeks to sow the consciousness of belonging to a specific land. But above all, it is a new paradigm that promotes and shapes community *self-determination* and *self-sustainability* through education and the defense of the social territory when it is threatened.

INTERNATIONAL RECOGNITION

Sometimes, during community self-governance, a surprise inspires profound happiness and gratitude. Other times, as in the assault on the Finca Madre Isla, a surprise causes of great consternation. That is why one must remain alert for the surprises that the struggle might have in store.

One night, for example, Tinti received a call from San Francisco. The caller identified himself as a member of the Goldman Foundation. He said that the Board of Directors wanted to talk to me. He asked, "Is Alexis available?". She said yes, but that the conversation would have to be in Spanish. After each member greeted me, they asked me whether I knew what the Goldman Environmental Prize was, to which I answered no. They continued asking me, did I know that it had to do with international recognition, or knew that every year they chose a person from each continent and one from the islands of the world, someone who had distinguished themselves globally in the defense of the environment. Again, I said no. They asked me whether I knew that the recognition was known informally as the Environmental Nobel Prize, and, again, I answered in the negative. Did I know that the international recognition from the prize included an economic contribution to the selected person to facilitate their continued struggle? No, I didn't. Finally, they said: "For the accomplishment of fighting for fifteen years to stop mining activities that would have caused an ecological catastrophe in Puerto Rico, for succeeding in transforming the mining area into a People's Forest, and for becoming the official manager of the first community forest reserve of Puerto Rico, we have selected Alexis Massol González and Casa Pueblo for the International Goldman Environmental Prize of 2002 in the category of 'Islands of the World.'" There was absolute silence. I was feeling suspicious, thinking about the many lessons learned over the years about money and its power. Once again, they asked what I had to say. I consulted Tinti, and the answer, which I will never forget, was the following: "Thank you, but I want to clarify that I don't fight for recognition and even less for money. I fight for the children and for the people of Puerto Rico, and my condition would be to accept not for the islands of the world, rather for the island *nations* of the world because my country is a Caribbean Latin American nation." Then, I said a polite goodbye and wished them good night.

More than a month passed. Then one day a certified letter arrived in which they invited us to the ceremony on the April 22 in San Francisco, and later in Washington, D.C., to receive the 2002 International Goldman Environmental Prize in the category of all the island *nations* of the Planet. I took advantage of the acceptance ceremony at the San Francisco Opera House to demand that the president of the United States withdraw the Navy from Vieques. The call received the rousing endorsement of the 3,000 attendees through their applause. Afterward, in the Kennedy family's home, we delivered to the representative of the President of the United Statesthe scientific studies conducted by Dr. Arturo Massol Deyá that demonstrated the contamination of the Vieques food chain with carcinogenic heavy metals. This international recognition was important for us and we appreciate it. Furthermore, it has allowed us to have the honor of meeting and sharing with esteemed activists like Fátima Jibrell of Somalia, Jadwiga Lopata of Poland, Sara James and Jonathan Soloman of the United States, Norma Kassi of Canada, Jean La Rose of French Guiana, and the highly regarded Pisit Charnsnoh of Thailand. This pleasant surprise was very useful in helping us continue our work. It also led to another and less pleasant surprise in Washington, D.C. ten years later, which I will describe in the next chapter.

CHAPTER 8

THE SELF-GOVERNING COMMUNITY
BUILDS ALTERNATIVES

Some of our sustainable developement projects: Café Madre Isla (1989),
the Forest School (2003), the Community Music School (2006), and Radio
Casa Pueblo (2008).

FOUR ESSENTIAL CONCEPTS

Self-sustaining Community Development

Community self-governance refers to the management of an organized group of people who voluntarily unite to overcome issues that concern and affect them. It seeks to defend the common interests of those who are looking to achieve a better quality of life and a better future and manifests itself in the defense of the environment, human rights, and gender equality. When a self-governing community moves from complaints and protests to forward-looking propositions and becomes able to sustain itself, when it breaks dependencies and develops independently, then it is practicing *self-sustaining community development*. Its primary ideals are self-governance, economic self-sufficiency, community-based social enterprise, participatory democracy, identity, collective property, cooperation, solidarity, mutual support, and one's own voice (*voz propia*), among others. Self-governance is a project in constant evolution in which the community seeks to achieve its own identified values. In addition, the self-governing community keeps its arms open so that everyone can participate according to their interests and abilities. This helps to overcome negative, corrosive self-interest. It reverses pessimism and heals disagreements. To be a self-governing community is to be *one*—one family, one community, one village; it is to live freely and assume the associated responsibilities. The mission of a project of community self-governance is to seek, through consistent practice, the transformation of the community's existing reality, and from that base, to generate social and political change. It is composed of a group of people who voluntarily work together in an organized manner.

Volunteerism

In community self-governance, the practice of volunteerism is the principle for its creation, direction, management, and evolution.

It could be defined as the 'work of people who unite selflessly to serve a community or group, freely and of their own volition.' They spend their time doing unpaid work with a humanitarian spirit and commitment to their cause. Voluntary work is a lifestyle held together by strong principles. It is a simple manner of contributing to the common good and achieving the organization's mission. Voluntary work can be supplemented by a core group of compensated staff who facilitate the volunteers' work in some capacity, but do not replace them. Similarly, the compensated personnel in many instances also contribute to the self-governing community through voluntary work. Keeping volunteerism alive in a self-managed community is a work of art drawn on a social canvas.

Community-based Social Economy

Francisco Salinas Ramos, in *Entrepreneurship and the Social Economy: Opportunities and Effects in a Society in Transformation*, writes that "the economic, financial, and identity crisis, with its grave social, political, and cultural consequences for so many sectors of our society, especially young people, women, and populations vulnerable to social exclusion, are opportunities for enterprises of the social economy in general, and co-ops in particular, to become agents of change." Here as elsewhere, studies refer to the concept of a community-based social economy as a form of community organization that considers and participates in all the economic spheres of action, from production to transformation, to commercialization, and even to finances. They explain that this view is not a recent one; it can be found in Indigenous communities throughout Latin America, and in recent years, it has started to become more visible in community-based groups, among researchers, and within academia. In short, a community-based social economy is the design and construction of an alternative economy based on communal logic and not the logic of capital. The community-based social economy distinguishes itself by the principles that guide it and the economic decisions it makes. A community-based social economy has a particular ethic, logic, and goal. The social economy is comprised of social community enterprises that grow and act with a social goal.

Social Community Enterprise

A social community enterprise is a project in which the primary objective is to achieve a positive social impact that benefits the community. It operates through the market, which mediates the production of goods and services. It uses surpluses innovatively to achieve social goals and manages itself responsibly and transparently by bringing workers, volunteers, clients, and other stakeholders to the table. Social community enterprises deploy business models to achieve social, cultural, environmental, and economic goals. Profits are reinvested in projects that ensure the enterprise's sustainability and finance the common struggle for liberation. They are run transparently and according to principles of democracy, participation, and social justice. They can create jobs and offer training that advances the common good. The principal difference between a non-profit social community enterprise and a non-governmental organization (NGO) is that the first aims to be economically self-sustaining, while the second depends on private philanthropy or government donations and directives. The social community enterprise seeks independence from the state and municipal governments so that it can freely direct its capital to humanitarian purposes through a social economy that aspires to build relationships of production, distribution, consumption, and finance based on justice, reciprocity, and mutual aid.

Casa Pueblo's journey toward self-sufficiency started with the introduction of the social community enterprise Café Madre Isla and the artisanal store. The revenues from both have created a limited community investment fund for projects with social, cultural, and environmental aims. Thus, the Finca Madre Isla, Casa

Pueblo Radio, and the Forest School were born. With the help of volunteers, collaborators, donations, and visitor contributions to the Forest School, the Finca Madre Isla, and the Cerro Mágico camping area, our self-governing community has advanced toward economic independence.

A social community enterprise relies on a business logic that prioritizes the common good and self-sufficiency. These criteria are the principles that guide our economic decisions—an approach distinct from the capitalist enterprise where profit comes first no matter the cost. Our business logic seeks to strengthen social ties with the community to promote volunteer work and lower operational costs. It prioritizes investing its limited profits in nature, music, culture, solidarity, and alternative projects. The logic of a social community economy is not dogmatic. It is a supportive economy from its inception, with a commitment to paying artisans right away, for example, rather than selling on consignment, and setting reasonable prices for our products. These commercial relationships have created links of solidarity and mutual kindness.

Casa Pueblo practices the logic of social community daily. Ours is not a traditional store, but rather a space meant for organizing and sharing. Patrons are not clients, but fellow citizens who are transformed into collaborators in solidarity with the causes of Casa Pueblo. When the social community enterprise expands using the principles of fair trade, based not on competition but on cooperation, it creates a supportive economy. Moreover, this supportive economy aims to build relationships of production, distribution, consumption, and financing based on justice, reciprocity, and mutual aid. Casa Pueblo's community social enterprises are fundamental for supporting its alternative projects. We have added entrepreneurship and the social economy to our previous equation of *science + culture + community = change and victories*, and, by doing so, we consolidate our model for local development in a self-governed community. The social community enterprise requires rigor and a continuous commitment to serious discipline, which, in the words of our doña Consuelo Lee Tapia, pause only for love. Community governance tends to minimize the question of economic sustainability and prioritize environmental or cultural development. Because of the rigor it requires, the social community enterprise may not be as superficially appealing as other key areas of community work like direct action or protests, but social activism facilitates its own continuity when it evolves to include a social economy. As Raúl Romero Gallardo has noted, "When a community, or system of communities, implements a self-sustaining model of development while building their autonomy, the process takes on an emancipatory character of great importance: they create community systems that are economically self-sufficient, ecologically sustainable, and politically autonomous."

MADRE ISLA COFFEE: OUR FIRST SOCIAL COMMUNITY ENTERPRISE

I remember the early development of Casa Pueblo's social community enterprise model. Café Madre Isla was born out of a great effort by a few participants in 1989, the first step toward economic self-sufficiency. But even though we had nine years of anti-mining protests behind us, it was one thing to have a protest, and another to administer a social community enterprise. The management relied on the resolute entrepreneurship of Ariel Massol Deyá, who had a background in business. The name *Madre Isla* comes from a volume of the collected works of Puerto Rican author Eugenio María de Hostos. Millo Pérez supplied the coffee beans and was paid upon delivery. Cindo contributed the toaster and the grinder. Ariel and I processed the beans in the Tanamá neighborhood; and finally, Tinti, Ariel, and I, along with some helpers, hand-packed the ground coffee with spoons, jar by jar. The artisanal labels for the products were designed by Danny "Pospos" Torres, and volunteers glued them to the jars. Late the night before the launch of our product, grimy and with the smell of coffee clinging to my body, I entered my bath smelling like the glory of a mission accomplished through community action.

Everything was ready for the opening of the social community enterprise Café Madre Isla. We celebrated the launch by presenting the play *Golpe de rejas* (*Striking the Prison Bars*) in Adjuntas to celebrate the release of the incarcerated patriot Alejandrina Torres. It was a production by Dr. Luis Nieves Falcón and the Coribantes Theater Company, with Roxana Badillo in the leading role. The immortal Oscar Collazo and El Viejo, reverend José Alberto Torres, were present. The play received the blessing of a nation that has been fighting to break the chains of dependence for hundreds of years. With evidence of the viability of the project, we moved from the local to the national scale, searching for support with clear objectives in mind: economic independence, job creation, and self-financing for future projects. The Puerto Rico Community Foundation (PRCF), under the leadership of Dr. Nelson Colón, approved a donation to acquire a windmill, jars, and labels. I will never forget my promise that "we would never make another request of him, because from then on we would walk on our own two feet." History is my witness, and I felt great collective pride when the PRCF in 2015 honored thirty "builders of hope," including me, as part of its thirtieth anniversary celebration.

I remember one story that someone from Mayagüez told me bitterly. He came to Adjuntas to buy Madre Isla coffee in a grocery store at the edge of the town, but when searching the coffee aisle, he couldn't find our brand. When he asked the cashier, she told him in a low voice that the store had separated it from the others because "it is communist coffee." To my surprise, and probably hers, too, the customer's response was, "that is the coffee I want, the communist one." Speaking of communists, it has been a few decades since we received a call from the Governor's Mansion ordering two boxes of coffee. After various attempts to verify the origin of this order, thinking it was a prank being pulled by a famous friend, a certain troubadour who has played tricks on me many times, I told the caller to go to hell. Immediately, the phone rang again. It was a woman confirming the order. A few days later, I drove my son Ariel to Calle Fortaleza to deliver the coffee, and, when I looked through the rearview mirror, I noticed that he carried a box of Café Madre Isla in each arm, and the back of his t-shirt featured a large image of Che Guevera. I said to myself, "these people are going to think that Casa Pueblo, in addition to being rude, is a bunch of communists, just like the grocery store cashier said."

There are many pathways to learning about social community enterprises. I remember our first experience with El Mercado Fruto de la Tierra in 1991, hosted on the patio of the tirelessly committed WPAB radio in Ponce and our dear friend Antonio 'Tuto' Jiménez. There, together with the Playa-Playita Community Committee of Salinas, and dear friends like community leader Nelson Santos, we started what could be called a beautiful first attempt at organizing an agricultural market based on the model of social community enterprise. I will never forget what I learned from the Self-Governing Community Dialogue led by attorney Enrique Ayoroa Santaliz and Aristalco Calero, who for twenty-five years have been training teams of people throughout the island to find solutions to dependency through business ventures. I also remember the twenty-two years of volunteer work by Aida Delgado and Confe Caraballo in the process of producing the coffee. Likewise, I acknowledge hard-working entrepreneurs like Jaime González, Graciano Papo González, Olga Pagán, Awilda Fuentes, Maribel Hernández, Maribel Vázquez, Gilberto Pietri, and many other volunteers.

At present, the social community enterprise Café Madre Isla consistently and efficiently produces high-quality coffee and has brought Casa Pueblo to a high level of economic self-sufficiency. It took us twenty-four years to afford our own coffee roaster. Now, we can complete the whole coffee-making process, from toasting to grinding to packing the product ourselves. Our bottling-while-hot technique, which creates an ecological vacuum seal, guarantees the freshness of the coffee. In this process, we only use varieties of *arabica* coffee beans cultivated more than 3,500 feet above sea level in the historic neighborhood of Guilarte, Adjuntas.

It is impossible to write about self-sufficient economic development without mentioning Tinti Deyá. She is a fundamental, eloquent exemplar of social enterprise and in all Casa Pueblo's other undertakings. She is the past and present leader of the organization's economic model. Her community ethic has made our dreams and achievements possible, and she has my most profound admiration. It is said that Puerto Rico needs more Casa Pueblos, and to that I would add: "and more Tinti Deyá Díazes."

ADDITIONAL SELF-GOVERNING COMMUNITY DEVELOPMENT PROJECTS

Energy Sustainability

The first solar energy system in Casa Pueblo was installed by our friend Emanuel Pérez in 1999. It was renovated in 2008, and in 2017, the system was modernized and now produces 100% of the electricity our organization consumes. Through the solar energy system, Casa Pueblo, including the Radio Casa Pueblo studio, has achieved energy independence.

Ecological Sustainability

Our ecological sustainability projects started with the community management of the People's Forest in 1996. We continued this territorial approach in the strategic plan to achieve legal protection and community management of Bosque La Olimpia, and the creation of Puerto Rico's first Biological Corridor connecting five forests: Guilarte, La Olimpia, and the People's Forest in Adjuntas; Tres Picachos in Jayuya; and Toro Negro in Villalba.

The Forest School

The Ariel Massol Deyá Forest School started in 2003 when 125 acres of land were acquired through donations from the town, the Arecibo Credit Union, and funds from Café Madre Isla. Ten years later, in 2013, the land became what it is today: The Ariel Massol Deyá Forest School, named in honor of its founder. The school has had a considerable impact locally, nationally, and internationally. Its success can be attributed to two factors: the curriculum, especially in science, and the use of nature as a learning environment for students to explore, investigate, and experiment. This new pedagogical setting surpasses traditional schooling. It cultivates the development of a higher sensibility and understanding of nature, with an awareness that we are a part of it. The school expects students to get involved in community projects. The community management of the Forest School is an integral part of the sustainable ecological development that we carry out, and it is a responsibility that we have assumed for the benefit of the entire nation. The Forest School relies on different specialists, including teachers from public and private schools in the towns of Adjuntas, Utuado, and Ponce. The Miranda Foundation generously supports this project. The school receives around 20,000 visitors annually and was studied and replicated by our friends in the Bosque Mo-de-lo Choco-Andino (The Choco-Andino Model Forest) in Ecuador and Chile.

The Community School of Music

The Community School of Music, established in 2006, is one of our emblematic cultural sustainability projects. Its participation in activities and events enriches the cultural life of Adjuntas. It transcends the local sphere, engaging with universities, towns, and communities elsewhere. About one hundred students receive musical training from six teachers, all with university degrees. The school's director, Hernando Dorvillier Hernández, is himself a product of our organization, who, as a sixth-grade student, sang at the People's Forest Assembly. The distinguished teachers are fundamental both in the education of the students and in the cultural element of community action. As of this writing, the faculty includes Eunice Mabel Santana, Gerardo Rivera Vega, Sergio Cubas Seguras, Shaemely Quiñones, and Jamilka Hernández. They are supported by student assistants Amneris Vélez, Nichole Vázquez, Sheila Vázquez, and the "big brother" students, Elvis Torres and Jean Rodríguez. The Community School of Music has its own self-management system and an innovative and motivational educational program. It is a model that practices economic, cultural, and educational sustainability.

Radio Casa Pueblo

Radio Casa Pueblo WOQI 1020 AM was founded in 2008 through its own initiative and thanks to an agreement with our friend Alfonso Tuto Jiménez, the owner of the historic WPAB station in Ponce. It began as the first communal and ecological radio station in Puerto Rico and the Caribbean. Its identifying jingle, "*voz de las aguas, los bosques y nuestra gente*" (voice of the water, the forests, and our people), plays every hour. Radio Casa Pueblo features educational, cultural, and environmental programming that transcends the space of the studio by reaching people locally and regionally, through the internet, and around the world. The radio station relies on commercial sponsorship, mostly from Adjuntas, churches, legal services providers, and others. The staff performs multiple tasks with a devotion to country worthy of Hostos. The staff includes Maribel Vázquez, Osvaldo Santiago, Bryan, Vitito Pérez, Carlos José, Carlos Medina and a group of volunteers including Vivian Mattei and Felipe Ortiz, and others. The following is a list of other collaborator-sponsors:

Brisas El Gigante, Clínica Dental Familiar, Cooperativa de Ahorro y Crédito de Adjuntas, Dr. Víctor Oppenheimer (veterinarian in Ponce), El Estudiantil School Supplies, El Campo es Leña, Farmacia Profesional, El Gigante Hardware, González Hardware, Osvaldo Hardware, Carmen Memorial Funeral Home, San Joaquín Funeral Home, Santiago Grage, Vips Graphics, Adjuntas Hospice, Castañer General Hospital, Hotel Monte Río, the Adventist Church, Carismática Ríos de Agua Viva Church, First Baptist Church, Jerry's Café, JJ Satellite System, El Kilate Jewelry, Jesamy Jewelry, La Bodega Express, La Casa del Agricultor, La Tasca Don Felipe Bar and Grill, Adjuntas Clinical Lab, Ailí Clinical Lab, La Conquista Laundry, Lucy's Pizza, Melo's BBQ, Abreu Furniture Store, Alcimeli Enseres Furniture and More, La Amiga del Pueblo Furniture Store, El Colmadón Convenience Store, El Deportivo Convenience Store, La Adjunteña Bakery, Parador Villas Sotomayor (Hotel), Tierra del Frío Restaurant, El Boricua Restaurant, El Original de Wiwi Restaurant, Vista al Río Restaurant, La Cumbre Restaurant and Bar, La Bellota Restaurant, and the supermarkets A Granel Express and Centro Ahorros.

Community Institute for Biodiversity and Culture

Casa Pueblo relies on the Community Institute for Biodiversity and Culture, founded in 2002, to administer sustainable cultural education. Initially, the Washington Irving Elementary School in Adjuntas signed a contract with the Institute to provide educational services to their students. The University of Puerto Rico in Ma-ya-güez also signed a contract with the Institute to facilitate visits for research and teaching purposes. Among those whose work stands out in the creation and organization of this innovative project are its overall director, Dr. Arturo Massol Deyá; Elín Cintrón, Director of the Adjuntas Public Elementary School; and Dr. Jorge Iván Vélez-Arocho, then provost at the University of

Puerto Rico at Mayagüez. To make this project viable, Casa Pueblo transformed the recently abandoned Washington Irving Elementary School, founded in 1903, located next to our headquarters. We restored it, installed a solar energy system, and incorporated an 80-seat auditorium, a lab, a music room, and an art gallery. In 2015, the school was registered for Historic Preservation, protecting the structure in perpetuity. Universities and public and private schools from throughout the country helped in the revitalization and transformation of this important site, and today thousands of people use it for educational talks and presentations on the future of community self-governance. In 2017, the municipal government and the Puerto Rico House of Representatives tried to take over the installation, used by the over 30,000 people who visit us annually. A swift communal undertaking in defense of the cultural education sustainability project stopped their attempt.

Partnerships with Universities

Professors from the University of Puerto Rico at Mayagüez, the University of Puerto Rico Medical School, the Pontificia Universidad Católica of Puerto Rico, the University of Idaho, Cornell University, and Michigan State University have offered numerous accredited university courses in collaboration with Casa Pueblo. These courses utilize the laboratory installed by the Community Institute for Biodiversity and Culture, the People's Forest, and the Forest School, which teaches sustainability science.

The Casa Pueblo Trust

Early in the 21st century, we set out to design a legal structure that could protect assets obtained through social community enterprise projects. In the search for institutional sustainability, we contacted the University of Puerto Rico Law School at the Río Piedras campus. Dr. Efrén Rivera Ramón, the dean, approved the research project, and several professors developed and later taught a course to study trusts that addressed our needs. This was a particular and previously unstudied topic. We were trying to develop our knowledge beyond topophilia, social territory, culture, economy, and biology into the realm of the law. A few years later, a student from that course graduated with a law degree, and through fate or luck, became a voluntary collaborator with Casa Pueblo. Insisting on anonymity, he led the charge in exploring the next stage in Casa Pueblo's evolving approach to community self-governance by establishing the Casa Pueblo Trust. The Casa Pueblo Trust was created in 2007 to ensure the legal protection of our assets and the institutional sustainability of our projects into the future. Thanks to the hard work of the people of Puerto Rico, Casa Pueblo's headquarters and the Forest School's farmland are protected and will always retain their use and character.

Rescue of the Historic Adjuntas Plaza

The historic plaza of Adjuntas is one of many special places for local self-sustaining development. Built in 1895, it includes walkways, gardens, two fountains, benches, lanterns, and shade trees; it is a space for fraternity and recreation. It is central to the town's identity, along with the mountainous silhouette of the Sleeping Giant to the southwest. It bears the name of Arístides Moll Boscana, a distinguished figure from Adjuntas, a poet, essayist, and writer who helped to launch, along with other poets, the Modernist movement in Puerto Rican poetry. On the south side of the plaza is an immense monolith with Indigenous petroglyphs known as *The Sun of Adjuntas*. The placement of this Indigenous sculpture in the plaza was the product of the Adjuntas Arts and Culture Workshop, now Casa Pueblo, in January of 1981. In January of 2004, it became known that the mayor had decided to remodel the plaza. The remodeling plan involved destroying the historic part, eliminating the trees, and constructing an enormous square that would have a monumental water fountain in its center. Casa Pueblo, in conjunction with the Parador Villas Sotomayor family, sectors of the town of Adjuntas, friends from abroad such as Ivor Hernández, two architects from the Institute of Puerto Rican Culture who persevered under reprimands from the Institute's director, as well as Amílcar Vélez of the Adjuntas diaspora, organized a battle and fought the plan. We won and saved the historic plaza. The conflict generated some tension with our fellow townspeople, yet what remains is the historic Plaza de Adjuntas, one of the most beautiful in the country.

The Adjuntas plaza was the scene of many years of happiness during our youth. There, you could roller skate, skateboard, and bike, and just enjoy yourself during the *fiestas patronales*, the annual festival to celebrate the town's patron saint. I used to play clarinet in Juan F. Acosta's renowned municipal band. We band-members played cards, ball games, and conversed with adolescents and adults about many topics during these Saturday get-togethers. I remember that Pepe Lugo, Chilo Nieves, and others constructed a makeshift basketball hoop to play in teams of three. You could also play volleyball, a sport in which I was not very distinguished, and the teams only invited me to join when they needed an extra player. One day, Tinti arrived from the University of Puerto Rico in Iván Ríos' public car. As soon as my teammates saw her, they took me out of the game and replaced me with her. She played on the university women's volleyball team, then Puerto Rico national champions. Speaking of Iván, in those days he ran a public car to bring passengers to and from San Juan every day, as well as the movie reels for Victor's cinema. One night we met with a group of friends in the plaza and he invited us for a ride in his car. It was magnificent. We got in and he took us directly to the garage at his house and said: "Wait here, I'll be right back." It took us an hour of sitting in his garage to get the joke of a man who provided a good service and was well-liked by everyone in the community. The hero Eugenio María de Hostos spent time in the Adjuntas plaza when he was organizing the League of Patriots. Gabriela Mistral, the Chilean poet, and winner of the Nobel Prize in Literature also spent time there. The memories of many men and women of Adjuntas whose accomplishments have enriched the island are also part of this plaza. All these collective memories were the reason it was important to preserve the plaza's historic character.

THE ADJUNTAS ROUND TABLE

The defense of the plaza, the continued voluntary contributions of the Adjuntas Boy Scouts, and the victorious fight against the gas pipeline that would have impacted the People's Forest and the Forest School set the conditions for the Adjuntas Round Table in 2013. There, Casa Pueblo signed a collaborative agreement with several businesses to commit to local sustainable development in Adjuntas. The agreement concentrates on five principal areas: community, economy, tourism, the environment, and education. It seeks to generate jobs, promote the use of clean technologies, and reduce environmental risks. Parador Villas Sotomayor, Hospital Castañer, the Equestrian Club, the Garzas Community Center, the community of Portugués, the Fishing Club, the Little Leagues, Boy Scout Troop 512, and Radio Casa Pueblo 1020 were all signatories to this agreement. I particularly want to acknowledge the work of Juan Ramos, Abraham González, and Domingo Monroig.

EVERYDAY LIFE

The everyday is a mirror into the secret origin of history.
—Ágnes Heller, philosopher of everyday life

While everyday life is the ever-present engine of community self-governance, it is often not given due attention. Everyday life consists of activities that are repeated regularly, including those activities that may not seem "important" or directly related to the sustainability of the organization. Through everyday activities, we realize that actions mirror ideas, and we learn and develop new skills. Everyday life is full of creative imagination. You make meaning by combining theories with practices and knowledge. Social change, before it is achieved, expresses itself through the tasks of everyday life.

Carrying out these duties is not easy. It requires management, technical knowledge, and coordination between paid personnel and volunteers. Some vital tasks, such as reviewing work plans, fulfilling obligations to others, streamlining tasks, and mediating conflicts, are quite demanding. Everyday life requires rectifying mistakes, dreaming, finding motivation, and growing to go above and beyond immediate needs. Promoting self-reflection is also important to help an organization's members take ownership of everyday life. Everyday life in community work is the force that drives social change, much of the effort directed toward setting up community governance. Participants create something new every day by breaking routine and bringing creativity and love to their work. Visitors sense it and say that they can sense tranquility, magic, and happiness in the air. The daily life of community work distills our hopes, clarifies our ideas, and produces the optimism that lets a social movement create change. The teachers, volunteers, and staff all shape the values of the people who work on the site, laying the groundwork for a more just future.

Day-to-day community life creates an ideal space for producing knowledge, shaping attitudes, engendering feelings of usefulness, importance, and visibility. It offers a space where people can contribute, offer solutions, live in the moment, enjoy themselves, and develop confidence in themselves to impact their reality and environment in positive ways.

LIBERTY PEAK

One of the greatest pleasures of community self-governance is having breakfast with the workers who wield the machetes, pickaxes, and shovels that ensure the sustainability of our projects. Whenever we started a project that required my participation, we would meet at 5:30 in the morning. We would collect our tools, discuss the day's work, and purchase breakfast at the local bakery. It was typically dark, cold, and quiet at this time in the morning. We rarely spoke or even shook hands. Then, one felt like a human being, just another person, present, regardless of one's role. We put Casa Pueblo's values into practice, functioning as equals recognizing each person's contribution. This shared understanding began with the kindness of a cup of black coffee, before setting out to do yet another battle against giant windmills.

I remember one of these battles at the Ariel Massol Deyá Forest School; it lasted about three months. We were building a path from the river up a stony, uncharted, and weed-covered stretch and to the top of the mountain. The purpose of our work was to provide adventurous visitors with access to a lookout point with magnificent views of our geographic homeland. The workers were like players in a symphony orchestra performing a joyous piece in a bright major key. They were happy, and I was happy to see how they were creating their homeland day by day. At 8 a.m., we stopped for the breakfast ceremony: bread with mortadella, cheese, and some coffee they had brought in a thermos. What a joy it is to share a meal when on a mission! While we ate, we discussed politics, conflicts, and our individual journeys. And so we began the conquest of the mountaintop. Breaking the ground, building the path, installing rustic steps, and at the same time, finding our way through conversation.

It was an arduous and challenging job. Week after week, the route advanced, turning our commitment into a reality for those who would come later. My GPS and the topographic map were left behind in favor of Ramón, Jaime, and Papo's intimate knowledge of the terrain. Devotion, perseverance, and above all, a lot of hard work with picks and shovels were humbly shaping our destiny. *At last, my heart, at last,* as the poet José Gautier Benítez once wrote, we managed to reach the top at 3,000 feet above the Caribbean Sea. To the south, we could see the vast landscape, the town of Adjuntas, and to the north, the Atlantic Ocean. Incredibly, I could see as far as Bolívar Peak in Venezuela, El Chimborazo in Ecuador, and the Sierra Maestra in Mexico. We embraced. With our emotions running high, we raised the one-starred flag on Liberty Peak. And since butterflies are part of community self-governance too, we planted flowers to provide the nectar those pollinators would need to grow and reproduce.

On the way back, I got lost for three hours and I found myself afraid in the silence of the forest thicket. I asked myself: What am I afraid of? Of being able to hold onto our reclaimed social territory? Breathe easier, I told myself. We have always managed to accomplish that goal since Casa Pueblo was founded. Ramón, Jamie, and Papo emerged victorious from that battle up their mountain and their footprints are there on every inch of that path. Through the invisible work of everyday life, they opened a way between Liberty Peak and a self-sustaining Casa Pueblo.

VISITORS AND DONATIONS

Becoming financially sustainable has become possible through another important component: visitors and their generous donations. In 2015, we hosted more than 35,000 national and international visitors, including tours of the Forest School and the People's Forest. Visitors generate jobs and support the local economy. Donations are an important way for people and groups sympathetic to community self-governance to support us. We feel very grateful for all their donations. One came from a Boricua living in the United States, who asked to book their wedding at the forest facility. We warned them that they could not have liquor and that they must comply with other rules. The wedding was held in total harmony with nature. Around then, letters began to arrive with anonymous donations. Perplexed, we investigated and discovered that the bride and groom asked for gifts for Casa Pueblo instead of gifts for themselves. A similarly beautiful thing happened when my dear friend Benny Frankie Cerezo asked that, instead of leaving flowers at his final resting place, people should donate to Casa Pueblo.

THE ACHIEVABLE UTOPIA

The present helplessness that has overtaken a great sector of humanity derives in part from our inability to dream and imagine utopias . . .

—Leonardo Boff

In 1985, we began the process of acquiring an old house to serve as the headquarters for the Arts and Culture Workshop of Adjuntas. The intent was to turn it into an independent cultural center, a place of communal coexistence, and a base for the defense of the land, waters, and people threatened by the government's mining proposal. We never imagined what would eventually result. We had only the will, the vision, and love driving us to do right by Puerto Rico. We had a dream of a utopia, which Thomas More defines as a communal, rationally organized society where homes and other property are collectively owned and where people spend their free time pursuing literature and art. A peaceful, just, and harmonious society.

Around that time, I came across an article by Pedro Zervigón published in *El Reportero* on March 9, 1983, entitled "No One Passes through Adjuntas." It appeared immediately after the Musical Poetry Concert with Américo Boschetti in the plaza, which we held to raise funds to acquire the old house that would be christened *Casa Pueblo*. In the article, he wrote, "Unlike other towns, no one is just passing through. Everyone comes to Adjuntas with a specific purpose." It has been over 35 years since that article was published, and what he wrote remains true: Adjuntas is a destination. Today, thousands come here from all corners of the country and from different regions of the world to support, engage with, and learn about Casa Pueblo and community self-governance. José Enrique Ayoroa Santaliz clarifies the concept of the "achievable utopia" when he writes: "Once there was a town, and in that town, there was a house. Today, there is a house, and in that house, there is a town."

CHAPTER 9

FROM LOCAL TO NATIONAL
TERRITORIAL MANAGEMENT

Over 30,000 people march in Adjuntas to defend the national territory
and to oppose the government's plan for a gas pipeline. May 1, 2011.

A TERRITORIAL APPROACH AT THE NATIONAL LEVEL

Community strategic planning with a territorial approach–initiated in 1995 with the openings of the People's Forest, La Olimpia Forest, and the Forest School–has been extended from the local to the national level with significant results. The local territories, building blocks of the Puerto Rican nation, are of the utmost importance; they are where people live, dream, and develop a national consciousness and sense of purpose. In 2003, and as part of our strategic planning at the national level, Casa Pueblo drafted and submitted Bill 268 to the state legislature, to establish the Fund for the Acquisition and Conservation of Lands in Puerto Rico. We carried out an intense campaign and saw the bill signed into law. It allocated an initial $20 million for a fund to be managed by Puerto Rico's Department of Natural and Environmental Resources to purchase lands critical for maintaining healthy watersheds. As we carried out this community strategy, local and national specialists like forest scientist Edgardo González accompanied us and contributed their wisdom, expertise, and volunteer work. At the time, I was still unsure if it was worthwhile to focus community efforts on changing government public policy toward sustainable development beginning at the local and rising to the national level. Now, the answer is clear. Since the law was passed, the number of protected areas in the country has more than doubled. At the time the bill became law, Puerto Rico only had 3.8% of its forest area protected, compared to 19% in the Dominican Republic, 12% in Cuba, and 22% in Jamaica. Today, Puerto Rico's percentage is close to 10%.

NEW PROTECTED AREAS IN PUERTO RICO

The community initiatives that led to the creation of the People's Forest in 1996 and to the approval of the Fund for the Acquisition and Conservation of Lands in Puerto Rico in 2003, have had a national impact and are of great importance to our watersheds and our forests. The following are some of the new forests and new nature reserves that have been established since 1996:

> Bosque de Cerrillos in Ponce (1998); Arrecifes de Tourmaline in Mayagüez (1998); Caño Tiburones in Arecibo (1998); Bosque Tres Picachos in Jayuya (1999); Finca Seven Seas in Fajardo (1999); Canal Luis Peña in Culebra (1999); Reserva Natural Punta Tuna in Maunabo (2000); coastal waters of Isla Desecheo in Mayagüez (2000); Las Piedras de Collado (Tetas de Salinas) in Salinas (2000); Laguna Joyuda in Cabo Rojo (2000); Sistema de Cuevas y Cavernas de Aguas Buenas (2000); Punta Yeguas in Yabucoa (2000); Bosque San Patricio in San Juan (2001); Bosque del Nuevo Milenio in San Juan (2002); Caño Boquilla in Mayagüez (2002); Punta Guaniquilla in Cabo Rojo (2002); Bosque Monte Choca in Corozal (2003); Finca Belvedere in Cabo Rojo (2003); Caño Martín Peña in San Juan (2003); Bosque La Olimpia in Adjuntas (2004); Tres Palmas in Rincón (2004); Ciénaga Cucharillas in Cataño (2004); Río Indio in Vega Baja (2004); Cañón Las Bocas in Comerío-Barranquitas; Cerro Planada Yeyesa in Cayey; Playa Grande in Dorado; Mar Chiquita in Manatí; and the Ecological Corridor of the Northeast.

Casa Pueblo's strategic plan, focused on territory and emphasizing forests and watersheds, has had a significant impact on our economy and other aspects of life in Puerto Rico. This is one of Casa Pueblo's emblematic contributions to the future of the Puerto Rican nation.

CONSERVATION PLAN FOR ADJUNTAS AND ADJACENT PLANS

Another component of our land-focused, local to national strategy was the *Conservation Plan for Adjuntas and Adjacent Plans*, which was welcomed and approved by the Puerto Rico Planning Board in 2004. This masterpiece of a plan was the work of biogeographer Alexis Dragoni and forest scientist Edgardo González, in conjunction with others. The plan's special feature is how it maps out how land is to be used, protecting some 64,000 acres in ten municipalities. In scope, it exceeds the total area of all forests managed or co-managed by the government of Puerto Rico, and is double that of El Yunque Forest, which is managed by the federal government. Significantly, the plan created Puerto Rico's first biological corridor by connecting five forests: Guilarte, La Olimpia, and the People's Forest in Adjuntas; Tres Picachos in Jayuya; and Toro Negro in Villalba. This ecological belt prioritizes the territory and its exceedingly important watersheds, which feed the Río Grande of Arecibo, the Río Grande of Añasco, the Portuguese River, the Tanamá River, the Inabón River, the Viví River, the Pellejas River, and the Río Grande of Jayuya. The Río Grande of Arecibo supplies drinking water to more than 1.5 million people between Adjuntas and the metropolitan area. All are tributaries to the lakes of Cerrillo, Dos Bocas, Garzas, Caonillas, Guajataca, Guayo, Guinco, Loco, Luchetti, Toa Vaca, Guayo, the Yahuecas Lakes, and Guayo Lake in Adjuntas, which in turn supplies water through an aqueduct tunnel to the agricultural reserve in the Lajas Valley. In addition, the plan establishes a fifty-meter protected zone around the boundaries of these bodies of water.

MODEL FOREST OF PUERTO RICO

The Model Forest of Puerto Rico was established in 2014 by Law 182, an initiative by Casa Pueblo in collaboration with many different people, planners, and groups. The law connects over 250,000 acres of land and nineteen protected natural areas throughout the island. Its preamble reads:

> In 2006, and with a vision of sustainable and integrated development, Casa Pueblo offered the concept of the Model Forest

to incorporate social and economic components into the biological, agricultural, and environmental aspects of previous protected area designations and initiatives. Also, that year, the Iberoamerican Network of Model Forests recognized that the practices put in place by Casa Pueblo in the protection and management of these forest areas are aligned with their philosophy. The Network also declared that the Model Forest and the Conservation Plan for Adjuntas and Adjacent Plans are models for others in the country to follow.

SUMMARY OF CHANGES IN PUBLIC POLICY

- In 1995, after 15 years of community activism, Law 1171 amended the Mining Laws to prohibit open-pit mining.
- In 1996, the People's Forest became the first forest reserve in Puerto Rico to be established by community initiative, and the first one to enter a co-management agreement with Puerto Rico's Department of Natural Resources.
- In 2003, Casa Pueblo secured the approval of Law 298, the Fund for the Acquisition and Conservation of Land in Puerto Rico. The law established an initial fund of $20 million and ensured recurring funds for the purchase, management, and conservation of highly valued ecological areas. It also linked the island's forests, including Casa Pueblo's Olimpia Enclosure, now the Forest School.
- In 2004, Casa Pueblo's Conservation Plan for Adjuntas and Adjacent Plans was approved by the Planning Board of Puerto Rico. It protects 14,000 hectares of land and created the first biological corridor in Puerto Rico.
- Also in 2004, the Ecological Corridors Law established land use rules in a newly created biological corridor that connects the forest reserves of Western-Central Puerto Rico.

The law aims to protect ecological processes and facilitate the free movement of wildlife.

- In 2014, Law 182 established the Model Forest of Puerto Rico and connected nineteen protected natural areas with over 250,000 acres throughout the island.

FROM ADJUNTAS TO VIEQUES

Our model of community self-governance began to have national ramifications early in our history, as evidenced by our work in Vieques. In 1983, Casa Pueblo organized a concert for that year's Fishermen Festival in Vieques, held to protest the U.S. Navy's presence there. This was the beginning of an interchange between Adjuntas and Vieques that continues to this day. The main inspiration for this and subsequent collaborations has always been the heroic example of the people of Isla Nena, as Vieques is popularly known, chief among them Carlos Zenón and his family. In 1999, we returned with Johanna Delgado, Edgardo González, Arturo Massol, and Emanuel Pérez to install a small solar energy system and we planted trees in the civil disobedience encampment on Mount David in the restricted military zone of the island. That same year, the first scientific study to measure dangerous metals in crabs was conducted in one of the military shooting ranges in Vieques. This scientific work led to other studies on terrestrial and marine vegetation, agricultural production, and goat hair, among other things, that together provided scientific evidence on the negative health and contamination problems generated by sixty years of military training exercises. Dr. Arturo Massol Deyá published the results of these studies in the book *Science and Ecology: Vieques in Environmental Crisis* (Casa Pueblo Press, 2000). Other scientific research on Vieques was conducted by Dr. Carmen Ortiz Roque of the Puerto Rico Physicians' Association; Dr. Cruz M. Nazario, Dr. Imar Mansilla, and Dr. Carlos Rodríguez Sierra of the University of Puerto Rico, Medical Sciences Campus; Dr. Jorge Colón of the

University of Puerto Rico in Río Piedras; and Dr. Carmen Colón de Jorge, among others.

POSTERRIQUEÑO

At the end of 2013, Casa Pueblo, along with professors and students from the Engineering Department at the University of Puerto Rico Mayagüez campus, began to design solar streetlights, or *postes de luz solar*. We called them *posterriqueños*, a portmanteau joining the Spanish words for "post" and "Puerto Rican." A year later, three experimental models were installed in Adjuntas, equipped with energy-efficient LED lights, and in full compliance with the long list of technical requirements issued by Puerto Rico's Electrical Energy Authority. The *posterriqueño* can last up to twenty years, which means it requires less maintenance, provides better public safety, and uses 55% less energy than the competition. If all of the island's streetlights were *posterriqueños*, the government would save about $100 million annually in electricity costs, and lighting would keep working when the island's electrical grid goes down, as often happens during major weather events like hurricanes. Replacing all traditional streetlights with *posterriqueños* would also reduce our annual ecological footprint by avoiding the burning 300,000 barrels of petroleum and would contribute to the planetary goal of reducing global warming gases. A few people stand out in this collective work of social entrepreneurship: Dr. Pedro Resto, Dr. Gerson Beauchamp, Dr. Arturo Massal Deyá, students José González, Eric Rodríguez, Juan Monroig, Bryan Rivera, Zulahilynn González, and Abimelec Mercado.

NO TO THE PIPELINE: EDUCATION, PROTEST, AND CIVIL DISOBEDIENCE

Dangers to community victories are always lurking. So even as we complete the daily work of management and administration of alternative projects, we remain vigilant to aggressive threats by the government or private interests. In 2010, when such a menace arrived in the form of a proposed natural gas pipeline, we quickly organized protests and reactivated the key concepts: *voz propia, identity, opposition, totality, tophophilia, land, the common good, social power,* and *community sovereignty*.

EDUCATING OURSELVES IN ADJUNTAS

The battle against the pipeline began with local education. First, we had to study and understand the project *Gasoducto del Norte, Vía Verde*, which proposed a ninety-two-mile gas pipeline starting in the south, in Peñuelas, crossing through the mountainous zone of Adjuntas, Utuado, and Arecibo, and continuing along the northern coast to Cataño. The pipeline would distribute natural gas from a terminal in Peñuelas, owned by the private company EcoEléctrica, to all its thermoelectric plants along the route. The plan was staunchly endorsed by the governor, the legislature, all governmental agencies, and the U.S. Army Corps of Engineers, the federal agency with the final say in the approval of the project. From the very beginning, it was a fight on two fronts: Puerto Rico and Washington. We educated ourselves about the pipeline to develop a coherent strategy for designing an argument backed by irrefutable data. To that end, we organized a Technical and Scientific Commission with specialists from different areas. Among them were radio broadcaster Victor Pérez and graphic designer Alex Massol Deyá. This Commission studied the project and produced the documentation that proved that *Vía Verde* threatened the land and water and put people's health and safety at risk. In addition, we made the case that the pipelines would not lower the cost of electricity; on the contrary, it would go up.

The next step was to spread the word. We held a press conference in Casa Pueblo on August 17, 2010, attended by television, radio, and print media. We presented our clear, evidence-based reasons for opposing the pipeline, and once the press conference ended, we began the first march against the pipeline through the streets of Adjuntas; students and communities like the Portugués neighborhood joined us. The press conference and subsequent march received wide media coverage and revealed to many people the negatives of the *Vía Verde* project, including the negative impact it would have on La Olimpia Forest, the Forest School, and the People's Forest in Adjuntas; the Río Abajo Forest in Utuado; and the Caño Tiburones Natural Reserve in Arecibo. It would destroy 2,500 acres of forest, impact rivers at 234 sites, and endanger 32 wildlife species, wetlands, and areas that produce 25% of the potable water in Puerto Rico. It would endanger the life and health of more than 200,000 citizens. The news headlines contradicted the government's media promotion. A few examples are listed below:

- "Forests in the Pipeline Route: Casa Pueblo Conducts a Technical Analysis of the Project." *El Nuevo Día*, August 18, 2010.
- "Taking Aim at the Pipeline, Alternative Casa Pueblo Proposes Using Solar Energy, Already Available for Free with the Use of Photovoltaic Panels." *Primera Hora*, August 18, 2010.
- "Adjuntas Draws the Line." *La Estrella de Puerto Rico*, August 19–25, 2010.

We reinforced the campaign with educational workshops throughout Adjuntas, as we had done during the anti-mining campaign. We held talks and conferences at schools, in communities and neighborhoods, and in the town's main plaza. On September 19, 2010, we held a successful protest march in Adjuntas with the participation of neighborhood organizations from the Portugués, La Olimpia, and Vegas Arriba neighborhoods; the Lions Club, the Boy Scouts, Parador Sotomayor, Castañer Hospital, the San

Joaquín Academy and other schools, and other civic, business, and religious organizations, including the Baptist Church. We made yet more headlines with these activities. *El Nuevo Día* published a story with the headline, "Thousands March against the Pipeline" on September 20, 2010.

PROTESTS AT THE LOCAL AND THE NATIONAL LEVELS

We conducted other press conferences, held forums at various universities, and participated in national debates. Every week, we released new information that kept the news alive. Our community-based volunteer campaign had the extraordinarily positive effect of defeating the government's campaign, which had cost them more than $3 million in contracts and media propaganda. The veil was lifted revealing corruption at all levels. On September 1, 2011, *El Nuevo Día* reported the following about the contracts:

> WASHINGTON - At the cost of $1 million, the Electric Energy Authority contracted a new company of lobbyists to try to obtain the federal permissions that are required for the pipeline project . . . In a deal with Wilmer & Hale, a lobbying firm with over 1,000 lawyers in 12 cities, the government of Puerto Rico can allocate more than $3 million for lobbying and consulting in the federal capital.

Without a truce or pause, we achieved unity among community groups who conducted extraordinary campaigns in Peñuelas, Utuado, Arecibo, Vega Baja, Vega Alta, Levittown, and Cataño, among other places. A coalition of groups like the Lawyers' Guild and the Engineers' Guild, universities throughout the country, students, scientific entities, environmental groups, unions, and churches, among others, reinforced the resistance. All of us worked tirelessly, and the participatory process strengthened the opposition to the pipeline. To bring all these many groups together for one event, we called for a national march in Adjuntas on May 1, 2011, with the participation of various sectors, including the labor unions. About 30,000 people participated on the International Day of the Worker in what we called the *Assembly from the Street*, in which marchers rejected the pipeline out loud. The headlines kept coming:

- "They Say No to the Pipeline. Massive Support. Thousands Ignored the Bad Weather and Came to Adjuntas to Protest in Opposition to the Project Vía Verde." *Primera Hora*, May 2, 2011.
- "This Monster Will be Stopped. Thousands Marched Yesterday in Opposition to the Pipeline." *El Nuevo Día*, May 2, 2011.
- "The Pipeline is Being Done Behind our Backs." *Primera Hora,* May 2, 2011.

CIVIL DISOBEDIENCE

Casa Pueblo joined protests in Barcelona and New York, where we also participated in the National Puerto Rican Day Parade amid the city's skyscrapers. The United States Congressman Luis Gutiérrez attended various activities, and from his seat in the U.S. Congress, he denounced the inconsistencies of the pipeline project. Though most people surveyed and the majority of social activists did not support the pipeline, and though our arguments had brought public opinion to our side, the government insisted on pushing through with the *Vía Verde* project. At that point, we shifted gears. On Saturday, September 3, 2011, we took our strategy of civil disobedience to Washington, D.C. Two of Casa Pueblo's leaders, Arturo and myself, joined with others from the diaspora in solidarity. The unionist David Galarza, and Carlos de León, a university student, participated in civil disobedience in front of the White House, and were arrested together with 300 North Americans protesting against the Keystone pipeline. Our close embrace with this progressive group was meaningful, and attracted yet more media attention:

- "Alexis Massol Arrested in Front of the White House, Denounces the Pipeline Together with Other Activists." *El Nuevo Día*, September 4, 2011.
- "Opponents of Vía Verde Arrested at White House Protest." *Puerto Rico Daily News*, September 4, 2011.
- "Alexis Massol Returns to the Island. No to the Pipeline. The environmentalist and his son Arturo were arrested on Saturday for participating in an act of civil disobedience in front of the White House. They also denounced the construction of the pipeline from Canada to Texas." *Primera Hora*, September 5, 2011.
- "They Return Stronger. Father and Son Arrested on Saturday for Civil Disobedience." *Primera Hora*, September 6, 2011.
- "The Massols Return from their Protest in Washington, and Announce that their Struggle against the Pipeline Will Continue." *El Nuevo Día*, September 6, 2011.
- "Massols Return after D.C. Demonstration." *Puerto Rico Daily News*, September 6, 2011.

The civil disobedience protest made a great impact throughout the country. It sealed the fate of the project. And so, from Washington to San Juan, in unity with community groups and organizations, we marched in protest once again to *La Fortaleza*, the governor's mansion, on February 19, 2012, and received media coverage:

- "Overwhelming Request from the Public. At the governor's mansion, they call on [Governor] Fortuño to put an end to the pipeline." *El Nuevo Día*, February 20, 2012.
- "Pipeline Protested. Thousands Call for a Halt to Vía Verde in Colorful March." *Puerto Rico Daily Sun*, February 20,

2012.

- "Overwhelming Message. Call Falls on Deaf Ears. Thousands march in protest to the pipeline project. Meanwhile, the government insists that it is the best option." *Primera Hora*, February 20, 2012.

In October 2012, as a result of our local and national struggle and our impact on the metropole and in collaboration with multiple initiatives by community groups and other sectors, we succeeded in forcing the government to put an end to the "pipeline of death."

FIVE ANECDOTES FROM THE VÍA VERDE STRUGGLE

Three in the Morning

Every struggle against powerful adversaries requires a lot of effort and sacrifice to succeed. The *No to the Pipeline* campaign strategy followed the general guidelines of the anti-mining struggle, but at a different time. Science and technology had changed, and with the help of volunteers in the Technical and Scientific Commission, we continually revised how to align that new knowledge with the community's interests and the common good. The struggle against the pipeline lasted two years. It was intense and required a huge effort. We had to be available 24/7, like the day I received a phone call at 3:00 a.m. from Dr. Gerson Beauchamp, a member of the Technical and Scientific Commission and professor at the University of Puerto Rico Mayagüez. With urgency and joy in his voice, he said: "I completed the calculations on the tanks, the volume and capacity, and found that not enough natural gas would make it to Cataño to operate the thermoelectric plant. What they can deliver is but a trickle." He explained to me several technical points which made the project unworkable from a technological perspective and underscored one of the main arguments we would use to defeat the iniquitous project. The proponents of the pipeline immediately dismissed the information as false, but time proved us right. As *El Nuevo Día* reported:

> In a letter to the U.S. Military Corps of Engineers, the Puerto Rico Electric Energy Authority recognized that the gas pipeline would operate at 30% of its capacity, given that the existing infrastructure cannot deliver enough gas for all the thermoelectric plants connected to the pipeline to operate simultaneously. (*El Nuevo Día*, January 13, 2012)

At the next Casa Pueblo meeting, one member said: "Gerson, you are my new hero; before today it was Alexis." I was happy because we are all protagonists in community self-governance, from those who complete the daily chores, to those who make the pizza.

Pizza

Wikipedia describes pizza as "a baked, flat dough made of wheat flour, salt, water, and yeast. It is generally covered with tomato sauce and other ingredients like salami, onion, ham, and olives. It is part of Italian cuisine, and popular throughout the world." In Adjuntas, we also eat pizza and my friend Juan makes a delicious one following a great, healthy recipe. One rainy September day, Juan and I were discussing the governor's recent statement to the press that "no one will stop the pipeline." For over four hours we had been discussing a new strategy to stop the unnecessary, corrupt, and disastrous pipeline project in the north, *Vía Verde*. Suddenly, we received a delivery from Lucy Pizza. "Who ordered it?" we asked the delivery person. No one. "How much is it?" we insisted. Nothing. So, tired and hungry, we opened the box. Big surprise: the tasty pizza spelled out NO TO THE PIPELINE with its toppings. Imagine that! This anonymous act of solidarity restored our enthusiasm that day, and we decided to organize a march in Adjuntas on May 1. You know the rest of the story.

The Flight of the Pastors

One day, I received a phone call from a man who refused to identify himself and claimed to have confidential information. As always, I listened, but guardedly. He informed me that he worked at the helicopter installations of the Puerto Rico Electric Power Authority (PREPA); they had started a series of flights over the *Vía Verde* route for pastors from various churches and other influential people to show them the supposed benefits of the pipeline. He offered to share the names of those who had already participated. I cannot remember what I said or did, or perhaps I do not want to remember. But I do remember that the press picked up the story, nicknamed the operation *The flight of the pastors*, and published the list of participants. The story generated a heated public debate and unveiled part of the strategy of the pipeline's proponents. Sometime after the news story broke, I entered Casa Pueblo and found it full of people, as it usually is. In the Artisanal Store, three people were buying Madre Isla Coffee. From their clothes, I could tell they were PREPA employees. One of them asked to speak with me in private and told me, "It was me who called you about the flight of the pastors." We hugged with the shared affection of militants who, in their different ways, contribute to the good of the country. This man's contribution to defeating the pipelines was significant, although clandestine. It counts among many other contributions, and we accept and value them all, including those from people who pray.

An Act of Faith

To continue the struggle and reach a happy conclusion after the failure of our first anti-mining protest that was attended by only one person, could be seen as an act of faith. So it is, with the caveat that faith is not only hope; rather, it requires action, work, and commitment. One Saturday morning, for example, a nice woman in her eighties asked me to take a picture with her. In a low and sorrowful voice, she whispered the following into my ear: "Please excuse me for not being able to participate in the march against the pipeline on May 1st. It is a duty to defend the present and the future of the people of Puerto Rico." She felt that she had failed and told me about the health reasons that prevented her participation. The confession impacted me deeply. In our conversation, I told her that hers was a good reason, and that there would be other marches and activities. She responded firmly, "Look, my son, the one thing I do is pray for all of you so that you may be able to stop that project." At that moment I felt a profound and distinct sense of solidarity and faith, faith as the substance of those things one cannot see but longs for. I responded, "To pray and to feel the most genuine desire to address this difficult situation is another way of contributing. You were at my side, accompanying me at the front of the 30,000 people who could march." She was thankful, I felt moved, and we said our goodbyes.

Several months passed. We celebrated our victory, and I remembered the phrase attributed to Bertolt Brecht: "There are men who fight for a day and are good. There are others who fight for a year and are better. But there are those who fight their whole lives; those are the indispensable ones." It didn't take long for me to remember the "woman of faith," and I thought to myself: "The indispensable are the ones who do not fight alone. We all matter, and it makes no difference how big or how small our contribution is. In the beauty that is life and community work, many small details are hidden from view." Struggles have many actors who fight and deserve to be recognized. Other invisible protagonists also matter, like that faithful woman. Doña Isabelita Rosado recently passed away, yet she will always be present, contributing in whatever way she can, just as so many others do. The same goes for Ariel, my beloved son who died in 2009 and who lives on in the profoundest depths of my soul.

From Casa Pueblo to the White House

"Tomorrow we are going to Washington D.C.," Arturo told me. "You go," I told him, "you know that I will get on a plane only if it's a matter of grave importance. But I can pick you up at noon." He hung up. The next day, as if nothing had happened, I went with my backpack to the Forest School. I was happily tending to some gardening work for the butterflies, when Tinti called because Arturo was waiting for me. "We're going to the White House to protest the pipeline," he said. "And we will have to partake in civil disobedience. We will be accompanied by good friends from the diaspora and thousands of others who are opposed to the Keystone pipeline." "Then I'm not needed," I responded, "there are already enough people." "The thing is," he added, "you are the recipient of the Goldman Award, your presence is important." And I told myself, "I was there once to receive an award, now I must go again to support the cause of my people . . ." That motivated me to go. Passing through security at the San Juan airport, the alarms went off and a group of security guards surrounded me. I asked myself how they could have known where I was headed? But it wasn't about the protest. In my backpack, along with my clothes, were the scissors for pruning and the knife for gardening I had been using that morning. That mistake could have cost me dearly in the eyes of my son. We almost had to abort the mission because of some pruning shears!

More than a thousand people were gathered in Lafayette Plaza in D.C. At their request, I addressed the crowd using megaphones. I spoke in Spanish, and an interpreter gave an eloquent translation. Boricuas and other Americans joined together in common cause, a lesson for the struggle. We were advised to leave the area in front of the White House and we disobeyed three times. They surrounded us with fences, while officers and their police dogs began to approach from all sides. The arrests began. All shouted like a hymn of unity, NO to the pipeline in Puerto Rico and NO to the Keystone pipeline. One of the officers looked insistently at me every time he arrested somebody. I told myself, "This guy really wants to get me," and prepared for whatever might come. With an authoritative gesture, he signaled to me that the time had indeed come. And as he handcuffed me, this gringo said to me: "I'm married to a Puerto Rican woman and she cooks so well." "*Coño*," I said with a grin, "loosen up a little, you're squeezing my hands too hard." This story explains, among other things, why in a photo that's hanging in Casa Pueblo, I'm laughing as I'm being arrested.

Crowds of supporters greeted us upon our return at the San Juan airport and the press covered our arrival as if we were heroes. When I finally embraced Tinti I coyly asked, "Am I your hero?" "My heroes are Gerson and Arturo," she responded wryly, ". . . and you, too." But I was only half joking. The history of our people is filled with heroic struggle, and its greatness will be recognized in due time.

AN INVISIBLE BATTLE

As a result of winning the International Goldman Award for the Environment in 2002, we reached an agreement with the University of Puerto Rico in Mayagüez to collaborate with us on developing more educational projects, forest management, and research programs, among other activities. The agreement also formalized the work that many of its professors and students had been doing voluntarily since 1997, when the Council of Management of The People's Forest was created. After five years, the university secured funds to create a distinguished research position at Casa Pueblo. Its mission: to implement strategies in the areas of management, education, conservation, and scientific research at the People's Forest and the other forests in the central island region, per the

Conservation Plan for Adjuntas and Adjacent Plans that we had designed and that the Planning Board had approved. The agreement would be in effect for ten years, and renewable after that for another ten years. A historic joining of academia and community was achieved, to benefit present and future generations.

On July 1, 2007, the journey we had dreamed about, one that was both necessary and urgent for the country, began with the opposite of a splash. The person hired did not come to fulfill the duties for which they had been employed. They created conflicts from the very first day as they tried to push their personal agenda for the future— not for Adjuntas, but for their teaching career in Mayagüez. This went on for six months, until the Dean asked for the director of Casa Pueblo and the Staff Committee of the Biology Department to submit their separate evaluations of the situation. The Staff Committee gave itself an excellent grade for their performance and proper use of assigned funds, recommended that the agreement be terminated, and that the person in question be reassigned as faculty in Mayagüez. The evaluation of the director of Casa Pueblo stipulated that the person had not fulfilled their contract, had caused problems by seeking a faculty position, abandoned their job, and did not produce the required work plan or research plan options. In December of 2007, the Dean of Arts and Sciences, Dr. Moisés Orengo Avilés, considered both evaluations when he recommended that the contract not be renewed. The decision was soon ratified by the Chancellor of the Mayagüez campus, Dr. Jorge Iván Vélez Arocho.

2008 was speeding along when the son of a teacher who works with Tinti nervously asked to speak to me in private. Visibly hurt and distraught, he gave me a document to read and sign. It was a judicial citation for $5 million against Casa Pueblo and two of its founders. It alleged libel based on the evaluation that we had submitted to the Dean, paperwork that was part of the agreement, was required, and was processed confidentially. After eight years of postponements, the libel case was finally heard in 2016 at the

Regional Court in Utuado. The plaintiff called as its main witnesses the director of the Department of Biology, a professor who had been a collaborator in the management of our forest, and the chair of its personnel committee, a defender of the environment. We crossed our fingers and returned home to wait for the verdict. In the world of community development, one must be attentive to people's intentions. Otherwise, an inquisitor with royalist DNA may appear out of nowhere and start dashing hopes. The whole process was painful, reminding us of the case of the undercover agent who betrayed Casa Pueblo with secret reports that did a lot of damage and besmirched a few reputations.

Two distinguished lawyers worked for eight consecutive years as volunteers defending Casa Pueblo and its founders. We placed all our faith in them, and they did their work with admirable rigor. Three months after the trial ended, the Court's decision came in: the professor's case was rejected without appeal. Thousands of pages of work, depositions, and legal strategy were put behind us. But it was an unnecessary trial that caused a lot of suffering. I give sincerest thanks on behalf of Casa Pueblo to the distinguished lawyers Luis F. Abreu Elías and to my beloved friend Juan. A bitter fight started by a dishonorable person destroyed an innovative collaboration between the university and our community and all the good it could have done for Puerto Rico. Nevertheless, during the years of our "invisible fight," we continued working with the same commitment, the Cuban poet José Martí as our guide:

I Have a White Rose to Tend (Verse XXXIX)

I have a white rose to tend
In July as in January;
I give it to the true friend
Who offers his frank hand to me.
And for the cruel one whose blows
Break the heart by which I live,

Thistle nor thorn do I give:
For him, too, I have a white rose.[1]

AN ENEMY OF THE PEOPLE

Sharing with visitors to Casa Pueblo is truly a delight. We learn together and we feel like family. We talk about so many interesting topics, like the psychology of liberation, Emurah, the parable of the Apostle Santiago on faith, Shakespeare, and the Zapatista Caracoles. These visits are truly enriching exchanges that encourage us to study things further and to reflect on our lives more deeply. In 2012, on the Saturday before Mother's Day, we were discussing the crisis in Puerto Rico and the world. At some point, Juan Delgado brought up Henrik Johan Ibsen, the Norwegian playwright and poet who is considered the father of modern realist drama, and who in 1883 wrote *An Enemy of the People*, a play that has not lost its relevance. In it, the protagonist decides to confront the rich and powerful of his town, including the media and the political establishment. He directly confronts the economic interests that value capital over the wellbeing of the people. For his efforts, he is made out to be a traitor, and many people in the town conspire to endanger his life. *An Enemy of the People* features politicians who lie and are experts in demagoguery. It unveils the corruption of those in power and the media who misuse the language of the common good to disguise their narrow self-interest. It also highlights the personal price that is paid when one fights for justice and a brighter future for common people. The plot is still relevant today and could happen in any place in the world, just as it did during our struggles against mining, against the pipeline, against the dumping of coal ash in Peñuelas. There are so many instances in our country in which the interests of capital and government have pitted themselves against the best interests of life and the health of the natural world. It is worth reading Ibsen's play a century after it caused such commotion, and asking oneself if it is still possible to ignore who the real enemy of the common people is today.

CHAPTER 10

FROM LOCAL ACTION TO GLOBAL CONNECTIONS

Casa Pueblo in the Global Network of Model Forests

Casa Pueblo hosts the Network of Ibero-American Model Forests with representatives from Costa Rica, Chile, Bolivia, Ecuador, Peru, Colombia, Honduras, Guatemala, Canada, Cuba, Dominican Republic, and Puerto Rico. March 9, 2016.

In 2016, we received visitors from the following countries: Spain, France, Guadeloupe, Germany, Australia, England, Sweden, Turkey, Lebanon, Japan, Greece, Belgium, Denmark, Finland, Hawaiʻi, twenty-five states in the continental United States, Portugal, the Dominican Republic, Mexico, Argentina, Venezuela, Colombia, Ecuador, Haiti, Bolivia, Uruguay, Cuba, El Salvador, Guatemala, Honduras, and Peru. In previous years, visitors came from sixty-five countries, among them Norway, Austria, the Netherlands, Kenya, Nigeria, Estonia, Poland, Israel, Viet Nam, and Latvia. How did this happen? How did we go from local action to global connections? The answers are many, but a key factor was our work with forests.

MODEL FOREST IN ADJUNTAS AND ADJACENT LANDS

Adjuntas means 'adjacent.' It is an appropriate name for a mountainous region that was successively administered by the adjacent or nearby municipalities of Coamo, Ponce, and Utuado, until 1815, when a group of families was granted royal permission to establish a municipality with its own government and church. I like to think that a similar founding of sorts took place in 2007 when Casa Pueblo joined the International Network of Model Forests, comprising thirty-one countries, as well as the Iberoamerican Network of Model Forests, which includes fourteen countries in Central America, South America, the Caribbean, and Spain. Our contribution consisted of approximately 64,000 acres, as described in the Conservation Plan for Adjuntas and Adjacent Plans (2004). With this step, a new paradigm was established in Puerto Rico for the management of our land. It is a paradigm that includes economic development, tourism, and sustainable agricultural development, alongside conservation and management protocols that incorporate communities, academia, the government, and civic, economic, agricultural, and cultural sectors, among others.

IBEROAMERICAN NETWORK OF MODEL FORESTS

In March 2016, the Iberoamerican Network of Model Forests celebrated its annual meeting at Casa Pueblo in Adjuntas, Puerto Rico. It began at the plaza with a march and a welcome by the Adjuntas High School chorus. On this occasion, we signed a collaboration agreement with the newly admitted forest, the Chocó Andino Model Forest in Ecuador, and the Network, represented by Inty Arcos. This agreement, exemplifying our principle of connecting local sustainable development with national and global action, would have repercussions in other places. In January 2017, Michelle Dorantes Palacio, a master's student at the University of Puebla, Mexico, studying Conservation Practice at the Tropical Agronomy Center for Research and Education (CATIE) in Costa Rica, did her fieldwork at Casa Pueblo. She studied the concept of the Forest School, and participated in an intense training process to deepen her understanding of the experience of the Boricua Forest School with the help of its students and representatives. After learning from our experience, Michelle traveled to Ecuador with the aim of replicating our model.

As of this writing, the Boricua Forest School has been replicated in the Chocó Andino Model Forest at five of its reserves: the Inti Llacta, the Pambiliño, a part of the Chocó, the Saint Lucía, and the Yunguilla. We received the following communication on August 28, 2017:

> The purpose of this message is to inform you that the Forestry Institute of Chile would like to implement, on a national level, environmental educational experiences through forest schools, focusing mainly on the sustainable management of native forest resources. We are currently in the initial stages of the implementation of our first forest school–in the Panguipulli Commune, Los Ríos region–and the idea is to implement similar initiatives throughout the national territory, and eventually generate a network of forest schools in Chile . . . We know of your ample

experience on this topic, particularly with The Olympia Forest School, and we are very interested in learning from your experience so that we can implement something similar here in Chile.

The Iberoamerican Network of Model Forests has now expressed interest in replicating the model of Casa Pueblo's Forest School throughout the Network's twenty-eight model forests in fourteen countries in Central America, South America, the Caribbean, and Spain.

INTERNATIONAL RECOGNITIONS AND PUBLICATIONS

- The Goldman Environmental Prize, considered the Nobel Prize for environmentalists, was awarded to a Puerto Rican for the first time in 2002, when I received it representing Casa Pueblo. The prize was given in recognition of our victorious fight against mining, and the subsequent transformation of the mining zone into a People's Forest managed by the community.
- The Energy Globe Award, founded in Austria in 1999, is an equally important international recognition for extraordinary projects in sustainable development. On June 5, 2015, the entry *Puerto Rico: Casa Pueblo Initiative* was selected for one of the foundation's National Energy Globe Awards. Casa Pueblo's energy model puts Puerto Rico, once again, on the world map of environmental justice. These two recognitions put the spotlight on the community path to renewable energy starting from local development begun in 1999. The community organization at the heart of Casa Pueblo received the two most notable environmental recognitions in the world.

In early 2017, two young French men stayed with us for two weeks to film an episode on community self-sustainability in Adjuntas for their video channel Les Vagabonds de l'energie. "PORTO RICO- Du local au global à Casa Pueblo" is the title of the episode, available on YouTube.

- *Résistants pour la Terre*, by French author Sébastien Viaud, was published in 2009. He records the experience of "exploring the world for a year and meeting the winners of the Goldman Award, ordinary people who are the bearers of extraordinary struggles," including Alexis Massol González in Adjuntas, Puerto Rico.
- In 2008, the International Institute for Environment and Development in London published the open-access article "The Evolution of Casa Pueblo, Puerto Rico: From Mining Opposition to Community Revolution," by Alexis Massol González, Avril A. Johnnidis, and Arturo Massol Deyá.
- In 2006, the same Institute in London published English and Spanish versions of the short book *Bosque del Pueblo, Puerto Rico: How a Fight to Stop a Mine Ended Up Changing Forest Policy from the Bottom Up*, by Alexis Massol González, Edgardo González, Arturo Massol Deyá, Tinti Deyá Díaz, and Tinghe Geoghegan.

JUNTE OF GLOBAL ARTISTS

Casa Pueblo established an agreement with global artists for a cultural project that took place in Adjuntas in the final months of 2016. An opening exhibition featured Baris Tukaman, the renowned painter from Hunter College in New York who is Turkish by birth and an adopted son of Adjuntas as well. Other artists joined us from Mexico, El Salvador, Lebanon, and the continental United States. The gathering of artists in Adjuntas (or Junte en Adjuntas, as we called it), began with strong potential to unite the global and the local. The concept of eurythmy (rhythmical harmony, from Greek eurythmos, eu- "well, good" + rhythmos "measured flow or movement, rhythm", a style of dance developed by the philosopher Rudolf Steiner) is part of the Junte. Its goal: to connect the harmonious movement of the paintings and the music with the natural environment.

PATRIMONY OF HUMANITY

The 2003 Quetzal Route, titled Rumbo a las Montañas de Parayso, took place in Adjuntas in recognition of the 2002 Goldman International Prize award to Casa Pueblo. Previous routes have taken place in the Amazon, the Orinoco jungles, and the Mayan, Guaraní, and Kichwa territories. As hosts, we received a delegation of 320 expeditionary youth who camped in the Bosque del Pueblo (People's Forest) over the weekend of July 4, 2003. After a march through the streets of the town's center, we celebrated an international party in which the Puerto Rican flag was raised alongside the flags of forty-three other countries. The newspaper *El Vocero de Puerto Rico* covered the event on July 8, 2003: "On Saturday, before leaving for Spain the following Friday, a group of 320 young adults from about forty-three countries who had walked the Quetzal Route through Ponce, Adjuntas, Arecibo, Luquillo, and San Juan . . . signed the Proclamation—The People's Forest in Adjuntas, Puerto Rico, World Heritage Site, Biosphere Reserve—to advocate for universal protection of these lungs of Puerto Rico and the Caribbean."

LATIN AMERICAN WOMEN'S ASSEMBLY

In August 2016, Casa Pueblo hosted an Assembly of Women Fighting for the Environment in Latin America and Puerto Rico in collaboration with The Latin American Mining Monitoring Project, based in Australia. Guests included the Front of Women Defenders of Pachamama from Peru, Honduras, Ecuador, and Guatemala. The first panel featured Lina Solano, from Ecuador; Elizabeth Cunya from Peru; Loren Cabnal and Aura Lolita Chávez Ixcaquic from Guatemala; Glevys Rondón, director of the Latin American Mining Monitoring Program; and Berta Zúñiga Cáceres from Honduras. Cáceres is the daughter of 2015 Goldman International Prize winner Berta Isabel Cáceres Flores, who was murdered for defending the environmental rights of her community. The second panel featured local activists, including Tinti Deyá of Casa Pueblo; Elena Biamo of Boricua Organization; Myrna Conty of the Coalition of Organizations Against Incineration in Arecibo; Angie Colón of the Northeast Ecological Corridor; Ela Cruz of the Karso and Caño Tiburones Area; Aleida Encarnación from Vieques; Elisa Sánchez of the Playas Para Todos (Beaches for All) Coalition; and Mary Ann Lucking of CORALations in Culebra. Two years later, in July 2017, Berta Cáceres' dreams were fulfilled with the announcement that the project that she had opposed at the cost of her life–the construction of a dam on the Gualcarque River, located in the Lencas Indigenous zone in Honduras–had been canceled, a significant community victory.

A PUERTO RICAN AMBASSADOR IN SOUTH AMERICA

Julián Chiví lives in Puerto Rico and leaves every September to go to South America. His route covers 10,000 kilometers and reaches deep into the Amazon Basin in Brazil, Colombia, Peru, and Venezuela. He was popularly appointed many years ago as Puerto Rico's goodwill ambassador to the world. Upon his seasonal return, he is received with celebrations of great joy and mysticism, and he takes the opportunity to inform us about the community work being done in our sister countries. He explains that he always returns in February because it is the month of love, his way of expressing the profound sense of patriotism he feels, and of making sure that his progeny is born with Puerto Rican citizenship. He is considered a great singer and is better known as Vireo Bigotinegro (the Black-whiskered vireo). His singing has inspired Juan Luis Guerra and Danny Rivera, among other famous artists, who mention him in their lively songs. His impact is such that the choir of the University of Puerto Rico campus in Cayey dedicated a song to him. We use that song to mark every hour of every day in our community station, Radio Casa Pueblo. Part of the song says, "Julián Chiví, Julián Chiví, the voice of the forests, the waters, and our people." Some people report that in the 1980s he organized different marches in conjunction with our birdlife, all of which contributed to our extraordinary victory over the nefarious mining project. They say that as part of the community management team for the Bosque del Pueblo, he was responsible, among other things, for rescuing the Indigenous ceremonial park and moving it to its original location. His extended family is recognized as a symbol of the liberation of our community forest reserve, a sacred social territory protected through community organization. Newspaper headlines annually highlight Julián Chiví's return to his native land: "Adjuntas Welcomes Its Prodigal Son," *Primera Hora*, February 1, 2002; "For Our Land and Julián Chiví," *El Nuevo Día*, February 2, 2002; "A Welcoming for Julián Chiví, Puerto Rico's Ambassador," *Primera Hora*, March 25, 2003.

This hero of community self-governance is only about six and a half inches long, has olive green plumage, and his chest is white or cream. His beak is black, straight, and wide; his legs are light gray; and above his eyes are pale stripes like eyebrows that are accented with a dark line. Julián Chiví is the symbolic bird of the People's Forest.

PART III

SELF-SUSTAINABILITY WITH A PLANETARY AGENDA

CHAPTER 11

A HISTORIC JUNCTURE

The Reality of Puerto Rico in 2018

Casa Pueblo strengthens the ties of solidarity with the Puerto Rican diaspora during the National Puerto Rican Day Parade in New York City. June 10, 2012.

Teach yourself, because we will need all our intelligence; inspire yourself, because we will need all our enthusiasm; organize yourself, because we will need all our strength.

– Antonio Gramsci, *L'Ordine Nuovo*, year 1, no. 1, May 1, 1919

Today, Puerto Rico sits at a crossroads, and the path that it chooses may have lasting effects for years or decades to come. Three developments define our current situation.

First is the crisis of Puerto Rico's political-economic-colonial status. The past decades have been defined by the ineptitude and corruption of political parties, politicians, and the government; the financial collapse of the government; the $72 billion national debt; the high unemployment rate; the lack of nutritious food grown locally; and a growing number of people in poverty who become more dependent on federal services every day.

Second, in June 2016, the United States passed the Puerto Rico Oversight, Management, and Economic Stability Act, which created the Financial Oversight and Management Board for Puerto Rico, made up of seven members appointed by the President of the United States and with special powers over Puerto Rico. The Board set the political relationship between Puerto Rico and the United States back a century by reestablishing direct control of the colony from Washington. The law also closed the doors to a process of free self-determination and decolonization and set the stage for Puerto Rico to become a perpetual colony. The creation of the fiscal Board had been given a green light a few months before, on December 23, 2015, in the Supreme Course case of "Commonwealth of Puerto Rico, Petitioner vs. Luis M. Sánchez Valle, et al." The question before the Court was "Whether Puerto Rico and the United States are separate sovereigns for purposes of the Double Jeopardy Clause of the Fifth Amendment to the United States Constitution."[1] The Attorney General of the United States argued that the answer is no because in 1898, Puerto Rico became a territory of the United States and as such, it does not possess separate sovereignty. The counterargument centered around the fact that in 1950, Congress authorized Puerto Rico to adopt a constitution so that it could exercise local self-governance, and in 1952, Puerto Rico did so. The question was therefore also whether those events transformed Puerto Rico into a sovereign state. In the end, the Supreme Court acknowledged that Puerto Rico exercised significant local autonomy, with great benefit to its people and to the United States, yet concluded that it remains a territory under the sole sovereignty of the United States and is therefore subject to the plenary authority of Congress.

Third, on September 20, 2017, Hurricane María deepened the crisis and exposed the depth of social inequality in Puerto Rico. The energy grid collapsed, disrupting the economy and people's lives, and the crisis provoked a process of mass migration to the United States, with its attendant dislocation of the Puerto Rican family unit. The emergency turned into a new excuse for the political and economic elite to advance their own agenda through the privatization of essential services and the imposition of austerity measures to the detriment of the most vulnerable populations, a process that leads to the impoverishment of many and the enrichment of a few. The impact was felt by all, and especially by workers in all sectors who were forced to pay the costs of the economic crisis. The process will be long, complicated, and marked by growing social inequality. This represents an enormous challenge for the people of Puerto Rico. Antonio Gramsci's call for intelligence, enthusiasm, and organization in the face of daunting odds and formidable power structures is still valid today.

THE COMMUNITY WRITES A GLORIOUS HISTORY

Every community in Puerto Rico met the national devastation caused by Hurricane María with exemplary community response as if collectively writing an ode to solidarity. Thousands of Puerto Rican volunteers, the country's moral reserve, immediately hit the streets, highways, and sidewalks to clear paths in solidarity with neighbors and rescued those most in need of help. It was not about being a new country, or two countries, or a country that had recently risen up. It was the same Puerto Rico that stood up as it continues to do today, writing its most recent chapter by overcoming adversity and surviving. It is still Borikén, just as it was during the Componte movement in 1887 when Puerto Ricans developed their own music, painting, and art. It is the same country that for over a century has proudly maintained its identity despite undergoing a process of Americanization that prohibited the display of our national flag for over forty years. That flag is the only flag flying throughout the island today, a symbol of our resistance and our fighting spirit.

Hurricane María revealed as never before the gaping social inequalities in Puerto Rico. Gone was the veneer of progress, and the poverty of the nation was laid bare for all to see, poverty imposed by inept and corrupt colonial governments that impose an economic system based on dependency, an economic system that privileges a few, and impoverishes the majority. The hurricane turned tens of thousands into refugees and caused catastrophic damages: more than a quarter of a million homes were destroyed, and the public utilities of electric energy, potable water, and communication collapsed. After four months, electricity was still largely unavailable, not only in the countryside but also in the San Juan area. Hospitals, hotels, stores, the industrial sector, and the 90% of schools that had been closed were all without power. At first, the government put the death toll estimate at sixty four people, yet soon thereafter a Harvard University study argued that the real tally of direct and indirect victims was around 4,500. Another study by George Washington University argued for an estimated 2,975 deaths caused by the hurricane, a number that was later adopted by the Puerto Rican government as the official death toll.

Corruption was rampant in the more than 2,000 contracts for hurricane relief and recovery awarded by the Puerto Rican and municipal governments. The situation reached tragicomic levels with blue tarps meant to provide temporary roofing for damaged homes and thousands of shipping containers filled with food all held up at the port of entry. The theft of goods intended for the general public by government officials was a disgrace that will stain the history of this period. Conditions worsened under the weight of decades of colonial mismanagement and debt. According to *The New York Times* (May 3, 2017), the total debt of the nation included about $49 billion in unfunded pension obligations and $74 billion in bond debt, funds that were supposed to have paid for the design and construction of a super-infrastructure that collapsed in the face of Maria. An arrogant, insensitive, and slow-to-respond federal government presided over the emergency, pushing the nation increasingly into an economic model of subsistence and dependency that has led to a massive wave of emigration to the continental United States: over 400,000 people have left the island since 2017, more than 10% of our population.

AN OPEN HOUSE BUILT ON SOLIDARITY AND HUMANITARIANISM

On September 20, 2017, as in every other town and city in Puerto Rico, Adjuntas awoke to the sounds of volunteer brigades using machetes and chainsaws to clear paths, walkways, and streets in the aftermath of Hurricane Maria. They worked to rescue the elderly, the sick, and families that had become homeless. Volunteers coordinated transport between hospitals and centers for displaced people. Owners of heavy equipment voluntarily cleared debris from landslides. Neighbors shared their homes and their bread. The "peasant life" of decades past began to reemerge. We witnessed people acting on their shared sense of identity, as neighbors, families, and friends, and even strangers, all started working together as a self-governing community. The initiative was organized to attend to the needy, without regard to who the recipients of the aid might be.

Casa Pueblo, built with solidarity and humanitarianism, shared in the pain and offered its solar-generated powered energy to health clinics for respiratory therapy and dialysis. Tinti was the driving force behind some new administrative structures that stimulated a surge in volunteers. Radio Casa Pueblo turned into a dependable source for the community, staying on air 24-hours a day during and after the hurricane. The solar energy that lit Casa Pueblo and our radio station became a beacon of light and of hope for the 2,500 people who had lost their homes in Adjuntas. The profoundness of the situation recalls the lyric of a song by the notable Nicaraguan songwriter Katia Cardenal on February 26, 2012 at the Bellas Artes Center when she dedicated her song "Casa Abierta" (Open House) to Casa Pueblo.

> Here is my open house / There is a plate for you at our table / Tree shade for your head / Open book, your life and my door / . . . Open house / Friendship doesn't question your creed / It pleases Mother Earth that we love each other / Without discriminating by faith or flag / Open house.

WHAT IS TO BE DONE?

What is one to do at a historical crossroads marked by the crisis of the colonial government, a modern federal dictatorship taking power, and the devastation of the country brought about by natural disasters? This is the great question now facing the Puerto Rican people. Such difficult situations can provoke pessimism and inaction. Some people hope that the crisis will bring about change by itself. However, a systemic crisis is not analogous to the collapse of a building. The colonial model has ways of implementing sufficient reforms to calm the general uneasiness and keep the structure standing. Others hope that politicians will bring change after the next elections, and in this belief maintain the vicious cycle of passivity. In regard to this issue, Casa Pueblo has practiced the following: one does not have to wait for political change to proceed with the development of an alternative model for the country. The alternatives can and should be imagined and constructed at the grassroots level.

The response by both the local and federal governments and the economic elite has been to take advantage of the Hurricane Maria disaster to reconstruct the island in a way that would extend the colonial model for decades and maintain the current energy system based on coal, petroleum and natural gas. The government plan includes the closure of schools, cuts to pensions and public services, and privatization. In other words: austerity, emigration, and the impoverishment of many. At the same time, several policy measures ensure that the island becomes a paradise for million-aires: deregulation, low corporate tax rates, tax loopholes, the systematic repeal of laws protecting workers and the environment, public posts with juicy contracts, rich contracts for construction projects, and the auctioning off of our territory and its resources. In her 2018 book *The Battle for Paradise: Puerto Rico Takes on the Disaster Capitalists*, Naomi Klein writes, "Thanks to a clause in the federal tax code, U.S. citizens who move to Puerto Rico can avoid paying federal income tax on any income earned in Puerto Rico. And thanks to another local law, Act 22, they can also cash in on a slew of tax breaks and total tax waivers that includes paying zero capital gains tax and zero tax on interest and dividends sourced to Puerto Rico."[2] A century earlier, in his poem "Facing History," José De Diego summed it up well: "Right through there and on the opposite side, the exotics entered laughing, but the natives still leave sobbing!"[3]

Casa Pueblo, in contrast to the government, has proposed that what we need is not "reconstruction" by outsiders but rather the transformation of Puerto Rico into the country Puerto Ricans want it to be. We maintain that we must move from this crisis toward positive change. We respond to the disaster with community initiatives that address the root causes of disasters and keep an eye on the horizon of an alternative future. Our response is based on what we have learned from our experience, and with those lessons we proceed, with more zeal, to weave our future on the loom of community, building a self-sustaining model of development. With joy filling our hearts, a fourth chapter of community self-governance begins, and so does a complicated process of co-evolution of being and doing. Again, comes the question: how do we make the change we want without taking political power?

THE PUERTO RICAN DIASPORA AND SOLIDARITY AT THE NATIONAL AND GLOBAL LEVELS

At the local level, a dazzling linkage of goodwill between the Puerto Rican diaspora and the national and global solidarity movements has sprouted creative networks that amplify our work. As the poet Kahlil Gibran tells us, "In every winter's heart there is a quivering spring, and behind the veil of each night there is a shining dawn."[4] And thus a new day began for us after Maria. We provided satellite telephones to connect families after the communications systems collapsed. We distributed tarps, bottled water, and provisions. We brought chainsaws and shared in the community labor of clearing streets, highways, and sidewalks. We helped health clinics distribute medicine. We even coordinated daily recreational and cultural activities for boys and girls with the theater groups Atención Atención, Y no había luz, and Agua Sol y Sereno, culminating in the theatrical performance of *¡Ay María!* We delivered generators as "community property" to centers for the elderly, homes for boys and girls, the Head Start center, refugee centers, five schools, and a small business owned by a young entrepreneur. We distributed 4,500 water filters. During this time, thousands of men and women from throughout Adjuntas stepped into Casa Pueblo for the first time, into its oasis of solar energy and love. Simultaneously, as if by magic or miracle but really through consistent work done over the years, many more individuals, families, and organizations came to visit Casa Pueblo from San Juan, Cataño, Toa Baja, Juana Díaz, and other towns. They came from further away, too: Oregon, Texas, Georgia, Wisconsin, New York, New Jersey, Los Angeles, Chicago, San Francisco, Chile, Uruguay, Argentina, and Norway, among others, to share donations and embraces.

LESSONS FROM THE HURRICANE MARÍA EXPERIENCE

In the path toward community self-governance we have encountered many sources of learning. One learns from regular staff members who work daily toward our vision, and also from the volunteers who then become leaders of concrete initiatives for change. These two groups merge into one and leave a trail of footprints to follow. I again encountered some of these footprints in 2018 with the arrival of loving supporters who helped us in especially significant ways. Here are some examples:

- A Boricua mother and daughter embraced all of us upon their arrival from Texas with a humanitarian contribution. I asked, "Why did you choose Casa Pueblo?" "Because I know them," she said proudly. "My mother would bring me here when I was a child." Lesson from the experience: Community self-governance is not fleeting, it is a permanent commitment, and it permits the integration of other actors.
- A supporter from Hartford, CT who had brought a donation in solidarity had known of Casa Pueblo since at least 2005 when he came for the inauguration of the butterfly sanctuary. When he saw the expansion, and the garden full of butterflies, he expressed with tears in his eyes how happy he was to collaborate with Casa Pueblo. Lesson from the experience: Community development projects are not like

fashion styles that come and go, they require continuity and efficient administration.

- A young woman from Los Angeles arrived full of enthusiasm, representing a group of Boricuas and North Americans who together raised enough funds to purchase 1,500 portable solar lamps. A Puerto Rican organization from Chicago made a similar contribution. Lesson from the experience: Self-sustaining projects are necessary to strengthen community sovereignty and to extend its social power well beyond the territory.

- A professor from Pennsylvania cried when she heard about the community's self-governing response to the crisis. She then talked about her shame that her government maintains a colonial relationship over Puerto Rico. Lesson from the experience: Many American citizens reject the colonial and indecent relationship between the United States Government and Puerto Rico, and they have become our supporters and allies.

- A delegation of three young people, including a Puerto Rican woman, arrived waving a flag we didn't recognize. They told us how sorry they were for what had happened and that they came in solidarity with a contribution to our community-based social project. A tall white man in the trio embraced us and said that he had come from Norway to Casa Pueblo to help in the wake of the crisis. Lesson from the experience: The accompaniment of global supporters is necessary and important for our advancement. The existence of local, self-sustaining projects is necessary if such support is to be properly directed.

- We had visited the University of Michigan, Ann Arbor in 1983, as part of the anti-mining campaign. After the hurricane, an eight-year-old Boricua from that city carried in her hands a donation of $300, the result of significant personal effort, and a reflection of the beauty of her family and her soul. Lesson from the experience: In community self-governance, young people represent hope and a generational relay not of age, but responsibilities.

- Three Haitian doctors provided medical care at Casa Pueblo. They cried tears of joy when we told them the story of Don Pedro Albizu Campos's visit to their country. Upon arrival, a taxi driver asked Albizu Campos for the name of his hotel, but he asked the driver to take him first to the cemetery to visit the tomb of the liberator Jean-Jacques Dessalines, where he paid tribute to the patriot. Lesson from the experience: We are connected to each other by our Caribbean, Antillean, and Latin American history and, of course, by being citizens of Planet Earth.

CHAPTER 12

AN ALTERNATIVE MODEL

Local Action in a Globalized World

A sign promotes our alternative solar model in the community of Callejón del Sapo in Adjuntas. April 1, 2018.

As a process, globalization implies the expansion of the world's capitalist system to be hegemonic and dominant, antidemocratic in its political embodiment, and destructive to natural resources. It creates wealth for some, better social standing for others, and for many, poverty and exclusion.
    —Mercedes Alcañiz Moscardó, Jaume I University, Spain[1]

Experts in globalization studies indicate that nation-states are being undermined by their growing indebtedness to financial markets. In other words, nations are increasingly dependent on those who control the strings of their governments' finances. Even countries that have achieved their political independence are moving backward, turning into neo-colonial hostages of the metropolis and global finance. Every day we see more poverty, starvation, food insecurity, and new forms of irrational exploitation and destruction of our planet's natural resources. There are diverse opinions about this reality. Says Rafael Sebastián Guillén Vicente, a.k.a, Subcomandante Insurgente Marcos, of Mexico's Zapatista National Liberation Army (EZNL):

> In the cabaret of globalization, the state does a striptease, and at the end of the show, the only thing it is left with is the power of repression. With its material base destroyed, its sovereignty and independence annulled, and its political status erased, the nation-state becomes a mere service provider to giant corporations ... These new owners of the world do not need to govern in a direct manner, as national governments take on the task of administering matters on their behalf.[2]

Brazilian educator and philosopher Paulo Freire expressed a related idea: "The ideological discourse of globalization seeks to disguise the fact that it is building wealth for a few while verticalizing poverty and misery for millions."[3]

In the twenty-first century, an alternative process of change has been launched in response to the barriers imposed by globalization: the development of a model of local community self-governance where the social and political change starts with the local community, a bottom-up rather than top-down dynamic. Researchers offer various definitions of local development in the context of globalization. For example, Mercedes Alcañiz Moscardó argues that "local development, without losing sight of a global perspective, is a fundamental tool to achieve, in the age of globalization (and despite how contradictory it may seem), a more humane, sustainable, equitable, and long-lasting development anchored in a specific territory."[4] This book, *Casa Pueblo: A Puerto Rican Model of Self-Governance*, has addressed some of the aspects of local development in a global context that characterize our model of community self-governance. Three fundamental ideas stand out from our experience.

- First, the model of Casa Pueblo is one in which we create locally, connect nationally, and project globally. We have exercised this tripartite approach to community self-governance from our origins to the present.
- Second, local sustainable development has a positive, measurable impact on climate change, forests, bodies of water, territory, biodiversity, health, and renewable energy. The local provides a perspective on the universal and makes possible the practice of acting locally and thinking globally.
- Third, weaving together local, national, and global practices involves reciprocal support, solidarity, and friendship, with dreams of shared planetary management and keeping a vigilant eye on the universal values of justice, liberty, and peace and their availability to all humanity.

LOCAL COMMUNITY DEVELOPMENT

Local community development—a process of social, economic, political, and cultural change that is both sustainable and located in a specific territory—is one of the most urgent tasks of the twenty-first century. It aims to procure, in the era of colonialism, neocolonialism, and globalization, a more humane, sustainable, and equitable world within a defined territory. It represents a novel strategy whereby the local community generates and builds its own momentum toward self-sustaining alternatives, all the while maintaining its specific identity. The process incorporates local actors in such a way that they become both makers of public policy and the subjects of that policy. It includes them in the processes of planning, design, and growth, and lets them contribute to positive social change. All cases of successful local community development involve local actors who are technically knowledgeable and socially enterprising enough to create a planned society without the tutelage of the state. A major goal is seeing to it that people feel they can transform their reality in ways that are conscious, participatory, and sustainable.

Faced with a governmental crisis marked by both corruption and by popular distrust of the political class, political parties, and the electoral democratic system, communities look to make changes through local sustainable development. As Arizaldo Carvajal puts it in his *Notes on Community Development*:

> Local development is a comprehensive development process that includes territory, identity or culture, politics, and economy. Its aims include the democratization of localities, and a kind of development that is sustainable and that rethinks the potential of the local territory and local society. Briefly defined, community development is an integrated and sustainable process of social change that starts at the community level, is organized in a well-defined territory, and actively participates in harnessing

local human, material, natural, financial, and social resources for the betterment of the community's quality of life.[5]

For Fabio Velásquez, to speak of local development is to allude to an assemblage of economic, social, cultural, political, and territorial processes, around which a community, drawing on their potential and the opportunities provided by their environment, have access to material and spiritual wellbeing, without exclusions or discrimination, and with the necessary guarantees for future generations to also have access to it. For his part, sociologist José Arocena argues in *Local Development: A Contemporary Challenge* that,

> [Recent] efforts to imagine alternative designs have led to multiple proposals that speak of human-scale development, of grassroots development, ecodevelopment, sustainable development, etc. These different proposals are attempts at overcoming the model of development that took root during the second half of the twentieth century . . . Local communities exist in territories marked by the footprints of the past. Space is never neutral, as it expresses the history of humans in that space, their ways of life, their work, their conflicts, their beliefs. Collective memory provides meaning to the relationship between past, present, and future, expressing thus the profound contents of collective identity. A return to the past through memory, a reading of these footprints to make sense of ourselves in history, is a necessary condition to action . . . The aim is not to identify footprints, but rather to identify ourselves in them.[6]

There is a great difference between the prevailing style of development that is driving us to ecological ruin, and the practice of local community development, which we are building and learning about together. The prevailing development model has brought misery and poverty to millions of people, all the while implanting the idea that it will bring us progress and happiness. It also proposes to maintain unlimited economic growth, proclaiming that having more is better, continually wishing for and needing more and more. It proclaims that it is natural for a product to be designed to stop working after a certain period, compelling the user to get rid of it and buy another, which is the capitalist concept of creative destruction. The logic of this model is that to progress means to grow, grow, and grow, and to always want more. It promotes the belief that new is always better, and that the old ought to be replaced. This model of development and unlimited economic growth puts us on the road to global chaos. Local community development is a better alternative when it is self-managed, self-sustaining, and self-determined. It is an alternative model that measures development holistically and not merely in terms of economic growth. It practices coexistence, solidarity, social economy, and continuous education; it values collective wellbeing, peace, and harmony; and it protects the common good so that all can share in the happiness.

SOCIO-POLITICAL CHANGE FROM THE BOTTOM UP

The concept of change from below refers to a process of social transformation that, like the construction of a building, begins with a foundation, and then moves upwards, strengthening the structure as construction advances. Such a process starts small and goes from the simplest to the more complex, like a tree that grows from strong roots. It is a process one must tend to daily, from the ground up, through concrete actions and revisions. This model of local community development challenges the pyramidal social structure where decisions are handed down from the top, where a small group at the top has the power to make decisions for the vast majority at the base of the pyramid. Local community development, on the other hand, is constructed from the base up. It looks for solutions and alternatives capable of achieving social and political change. Building from the bottom up requires a distinct logic: community logic, rather than the logic of capital. It focuses on changes at the community level, not at the level of political parties or governments. It encourages people to be protagonists rather than spectators. Individuals and their communities turn themselves into creators and transformers of society. They become social actors who do not belong to the power elite, an elite that uses crises as opportunities to enrich and entrench itself by privatizing essential social services, imposing austerity measures that negatively affect the most vulnerable populations and introducing reforms that generate passive discontent. Local community development "from the bottom up, toward social and political change" refers both to the struggle against powerful and predatory interests and to the growth of social consciousness that inspires action and transformation. Local development leads to empowerment and self-governance and breaks the cycle of dependency. It generates social changes, and in the process, builds political power.

ACCOMPANIMENT

The concept of accompaniment in local community development means that community members and external players who can provide their knowledge and skillsets connect with each other. In successfully advancing local development, a variety of communities and sectors at the national and global levels provide crucial accompaniment to the local struggle. This concept, which had been materializing and growing for years at Casa Pueblo, erupted in an impressive bonfire of love after Hurricane María, with the accompaniment of the Puerto Rican diaspora, and the outpouring of support by national and global groups.

SOCIAL COMMUNITY PACT

A social community pact can be defined as an agreed-upon partnership between local actors, local organizations, and local social groups to link one another's diverse efforts, abilities, and interests in ways that are complementary and advance common goals. This pact, which can be understood as a process of exchanges and interconnections, includes agreements and associations that work symbiotically to grow local community development projects. Social community pacts are a viable and unitary path to achieving real change in the community, and they build trust.

SOCIAL POWER

The concept of the social power of Casa Pueblo aligns with the thinking of prominent Puerto Rican educator and independence advocate Eugenio María de Hostos. He wrote that social power ". . . is the opposite of power under colonialism. Instead of using it to accumulate political power at the top, it is used to increase the power of the base. Instead of aiming for the dominance of the many by the few, it aims for the mastery of individuals over themselves. Instead of endeavoring to fabricate political parties out of thin air, it goes out of its way to cement in the consciousness of our sad homeland the notion that we have rights, a knowledge of our duties, and the acknowledgment of our responsibilities." At Casa Pueblo, social power manifests itself in the independence of our decisions in support of the common good. Our social power relies on the moral reserve of the Puerto Rican people, the real protagonist of our victories, as evidenced by their determined and massive support of our struggles and eventual triumphs against mining (1995), the gas pipeline (2012), and the municipal and legislative attempts to seize the old school grounds (2017) that we have used for over fifteen years as the site of our Community School of Music, Art Gallery, and more recently our Solar Cinema. We see social power in the transformation of the proposed mining zone into a forest reserve managed by the community for over twenty years now. We feel it when we achieve significant changes in public policy. The strengthening of social power is vitally important if we want to protect the gains and the growth of self-sustainable community development.

COMMUNITY SOVEREIGNTY

The concept of community sovereignty refers to the power and the liberty of a self-governing organization to make decisions for itself, to set its own goals, and to undertake its own alternative projects. It is a concept in continual construction, with a committed and consistent practice in community self-governance rooted in the common good. It is acting with independence and in accordance with one's standards when developing community policies. In the face of an obsolete system that does not serve the country well, community sovereignty slowly generates the ideological principles of an alternative society. Casa Pueblo's political model is one of self-governance, sustainability, and community self-determination. Put into practice via the intertwined concepts of positions, struggles, and concrete projects, we define community sovereignty. Community sovereignty manifests itself as economic self-sufficiency via projects like our Madre Isla Coffee, our artisanal store, and similar initiatives that increase our community's freedom. This is all amplified through the exercise of energy, ecological, educational, and cultural sovereignty, as well as through self-sustaining local projects like the Forest School, the Community Music School, Casa Pueblo Radio, and Casa Pueblo Solar. At this historical juncture that is Puerto Rico in 2018, Casa Pueblo continues to work toward community sovereignty, without the interference of political parties or governments, to make a qualitative and quantitative leap in local community development.

MORAL BEAUTY

The lived experience in the house of community self-governance (a house that is at once humanitarian, caring, and alternative) obliges me to add some final remarks. It so happens that in April 2018 we offered a university course at Casa Pueblo called Advances in Microbial Ecology. The course, taught by Dr. Larry Forney and Dr. Eva Top of the University of Idaho, and Dr. Arturo Massol Deyá of the University of Puerto Rico Mayagüez, is part of a self-governing educational system that has been active for fourteen consecutive years. At the end of the course, I had the opportunity to ask the enthusiastic students: "How do you feel after the intense educational journey that included fieldwork in the Forest School and the People's Forest?" I was curious about what moves so many people–like those who visit and engage with us–to feel happiness and attachment for our self-governing projects and to make our dreams their own? What is it that moves them to bid us farewell with hugs, smiles, expressing their hopes of returning? The students responded, speaking about Casa Pueblo's work formula, which combines science, culture, and community as the basic elements to produce change. They expressed that they sensed peace, tenderness, passion, and energy; they perceived justice, self-governance, self-esteem, and the work of liberation. They said that they were grateful for the attention they received and our commitment to our community and our environment. They were surprised by our achievements, they fell in love with the project, and the initiative made them want to return and be part of the community's self-governance. They said they were happy working with us. As time passed and I reflected on the experience, I kept thinking that there must be an explanation to summarize these feelings. Finally, I found the words to express it: moral beauty. Moral beauty is engaging in positive activities and doing good. It is the practice of loving one's fellow beings. It is fighting for justice, equality, and social transformation. Moral beauty constitutes working for the common good in specific, local ways while contemplating the universal dimension of that work. It is the beauty of the good that should be made into a work of art, into a masterpiece; the brighter a work of moral beauty shines, the greater the happiness one feels.

"And what is the supreme good of humankind?" asks Augusto Boal in *Theater of the Oppressed*. "Happiness!," he replies, noting that "each human action is limited in scope, but all the actions together have as their ultimate goal the supreme good of humankind."[7]

CHAPTER 13

ENERGY SOVEREIGNTY

A Common Solar Energy Project for
Adjuntas and Adjacent Lands

A community mural celebrates the progress of our energy projects in Adjuntas and its neighborhoods. September 2018.

And so, from this moment and this point onwards, progress begins to expand from below, upwards, and to the sides in accordance with a capillary process, just as in the physics of fluids.

– Sergio Boisier[1]

Through the alchemy of community praxis, we have been forging a Common Solar Energy Project for Adjuntas and Adjacent Lands. It began with the important step of vanquishing the threat of mining, disguised as "development." We then focused on our social territory, treating our forests and water as common goods. Finally, we began building alternative self-sustaining development projects born out of community self-governance. Through this Common Project, we seek to advance a kind of local development that resonates throughout Puerto Rico and becomes a replicable model to addresses energy, economic, territorial, and cultural issues, always with the goal of empowering communities to elevate their quality of life and wellbeing. This requires the support of local, national, and global actors so that we can uplift each other. This is not about the creation of a political party "of the people." Instead, it is a collective experiment that moves toward socio-political change from a starting point of solidarity and commitment.

THE ENERGY INSURRECTION

The energy insurrection began at latitude 18°9' N and longitude 66°43' W on May 15, 1999, when we installed a modest photovoltaic solar system at Casa Pueblo. In 2008, this model gained renewed life with the approval in Puerto Rico of "net metering", a billing mechanism that credits owners of solar energy systems for the electricity they add to the grid operated by Puerto Rico's Electric Energy Authority (AEE). The insurrection was also made possible thanks to the strong support of the Department of Electrical

Engineering at the University of Puerto Rico Mayagüez, which provided the solar panels and technical assistance by engineers Gelson Beauchamp, Efraín O'Neill, Gerardo Cosme, student René Zamot, and Dr. Arturo Massol Deyá. The project gained national attention when it was awarded the Important Work in Electrical Engineering prize in 2008 by the Association of Engineers and Surveyors of Puerto Rico.

Casa Pueblo's solar energy system was modernized in 2017 and it now produces more energy than we consume. In this way, we added energy sovereignty to the media sovereignty we had already achieved with our radio station's studios. In other words, we now understood energy sovereignty as our self-governing community's ability to generate all of the energy it consumes. This was a radical change in community self-determination considering the systems put in place by oligopolies and governments to keep us dependent on coal, petroleum, and natural gas to generate electricity in Puerto Rico. After ten years of stalling, in October of 2018, the AEE finally implemented the model of net metering. This allowed us to sell the 25% of excess energy we generated that year back to the national grid and to earn additional revenue for Casa Pueblo. Another important step at the national level was the successful fight to stop a gas pipeline (2010-2012) that would have forced the country to depend on imported gas to generate electricity. This victory was another community milestone in our fight for renewable energy and against the domination of fossil fuels.

After Hurricane María struck in 2017 and demonstrated the fragility of the national power grid and the urgent needs of the community, Casa Pueblo launched a new workshop on solar energy. The community's bottom-up approach, masterfully led by the associate director Arturo Massol Deyá, produced extraordinary work at the local, national and international levels. The Casa Pueblo collective played a unifying role by working daily with local communities. We welcomed hundreds of visitors, international journalists, and groups from all over Puerto Rico who came to learn how we articulated and practiced this innovative strategy. We received a commission of fifteen congressperson from the United States, and we also participated in different forums with institutions such as Princeton University, Brown University, UMass Amherst, the Ecological Society of America (New Orleans), the Global Climate Action Summit (San Francisco), the University of Notre Dame, Rutgers University, and the American Museum of Natural History in New York. From this work emerged a round table dialogue with sectors of the Puerto Rican diaspora and with groups at the national and global levels. The energy insurrection had initiated its first large-scale project based on local self-sustaining development: the Solar Belt in Adjuntas and Adjoining Lands.

SOLAR BELT

The process of planning, designing, and implementing the Solar Belt has required arduous, urgent, and coordinated efforts. Selecting the most in-need and eco-friendly families in remote locations where the sun can provide power and address needs is a task for extraordinary people who possess an elevated social consciousness. Widespread human suffering becomes a part of a person. It is one thing to see it in televised reports and documentaries, but it is another to witness it first-hand with the people up in the mountains. Their suffering fills the heart and spirit with indignation. The project was carried out with new volunteers and personnel who regularly carried out multiple daily tasks to fulfill their rigorous "devotion to the duty," in the words of the great teacher Eugenio María de Hostos. Patiently impatient, we keep working to build a Community Solar Belt that powers seventeen neighborhoods, including the Aduntas town center. The practice of energy sovereignty takes on a new dimension when the community can manage the production of its own power. The Solar Belt project has created a rainbow of hopes and promises, with the clear understanding that individual interests are subject to the interests of the common good. We designed talks and training materials on solar energy systems so that community members could fulfill their technical assistance and maintenance needs. Our objective was clear: not simply to help but to train communities to break their dependence on fossil fuels. And there was light, thanks to the rays of Brother Sun! Here are some of the results:

- Solar lamps and education on renewables. Five months after Hurricane María, we had distributed solar lamps to about 75% of the population of Adjuntas, to hundreds of visitors from diverse municipalities, and to high-need municipalities like Vieques, Loíza, La Perla, Yauco, Salinas, Utuado, Jayuya, Villa Sin Miedo, Canóvanas, and Lares.
- A solar-based model for urgent health care. The community strategy entered a second phase when we implemented an urgent health care model during November and December of 2017. It began with ten homes in Ballajá in the sector of El Hoyo, Adjuntas where the residents needed respiratory therapy and dialysis. Later, five of these homes received permanent solar systems.
- A solar model in the home for food security. High-efficiency (RB) solar refrigerators were next: a total of fifty-four systems were installed in all seventeen neighborhoods of Adjuntas.
- A solar model of economic activation. This process began in January 2018. We installed solar systems in five shops in isolated areas in Guilarte, La Olimpia, Vegas Abajo, Tanamá, a bakery on the way to Guilarte, and the pizzeria El Campo es Leña in the mining zone. The model of economic activation also included in this project the downtown, installing solar systems at the Pérez Barbershop, the Vista del Río restaurant, the Agro-center, and the hardware stores Papún and El Gigante.
- 100% solar-powered houses. We made other agreements

with the Puerto Rican diaspora and with institutional donors. Thirty-one homes and structures went solar, like cucubanos or fireflies: Barrio Tanamá and Barrio Guilarte; the Solar Corridors at the Forest School in La Olimpia neighborhood; Finca Madre Isla in the Vacas Saltillo neighborhood; the People's Forest in the neighborhoods of Vegas Abajo, Juan González, and Pellejas; the Callejón del Sapo Community's Solar Alleyway in the town center; La Playita; and the home of Doña Martina on Water Street.

CASA PUEBLO EVOLVES AGAIN

Just as it had in earlier phases, Casa Pueblo once again evolved, and the energy insurrection fortified other self-sustaining projects. Here are a few:

- Solar cinema. As part of the thirty-eighth anniversary of Casa Pueblo in 2018, we opened the first solar cinema in Puerto Rico. The project seeks to advance social and energy transformation through educational entertainment. The cinema has seventy-one seats and is equipped with a big screen, a Dolby 7.1 sound system, and a high-definition projector. Additionally, it features a mural by master artist Antonio Martorell: on a background of gray felt, we are led through an iconic mountainous landscape filled with faces of community members who are part of Casa Pueblo. The Adjuntan filmmakers Alejandro Wolfe and Rhett Lee García help manage the Solar Cinema.
- Solar microgrids. The microgrids are interconnected in a network that functions independently from the national network. The generation and storage sources are close to the microgrid connections to provide easy access for service. A microgrid, for example, links Casa Pueblo, Radio Casa Pueblo, the apartment in the upper level, and the

Solar Cinema.

- The new solar classroom. After Hurricane María destroyed the classroom in the Ariel Massol Deyá Forest School, we constructed a new one with a modern photovoltaic solar system.
- Radio Casa Pueblo is 100% solar. On January 16, 2018, our community radio station became the only one in the Caribbean to achieve total energy independence from the national grid, thanks to a solar system that provides power to the transmitter and the antenna in the La Olimpia neighborhood of Adjuntas.
- Satellite communication. On June 1, 2018, Radio Casa Pueblo installed new infrastructure that will permit it to provide continued transmissions via satellite if the transmitter and antenna are affected by hurricanes or other contingencies.

We began 2019 with additional solar projects in critical places that must remain operational no matter what: Mercy Home for Elders, the local emergency room, and the local fire station. Casa Pueblo entered its thirty-ninth year ready to launch a national campaign, 50% with the Sun, and we continue raising "dreams and kites" of liberty, as the Puerto Rican national hero José de Diego taught us.

ADJUNTAS SOLAR TOWN

For our thirty-ninth anniversary on April 21, 2019, we gathered with multiple sectors of the Adjuntas community, national groups, and international personalities. Thousands of citizens participated in the March of the Sun to demand that the government break its dependency on oil, coal, and natural gas and move instead toward a model of renewable energy for the country. On that day, we applied the principle from protest to propositions (without discarding protest) when we announced a major new project for community-based energy generation and distribution, one to change the energy paradigm in Puerto Rico and use solar energy to power the urban core of Adjuntas. The project aims to reduce the cost of energy, activate the economy, build resilience, and initiate a green fund that will help the town grow through energy independence. A new actor has joined Casa Pueblo for this project: Alex Honnold, the first person to free solo climb El Capitan in Yosemite, California. His feat was filmed, and the resulting documentary *Free Solo* (directed by E. Chai Vasarhelyi, 2018) won an Oscar for best documentary. The Honnold Foundation, based in San Francisco, is accompanying us and a core group of local merchants in our mission to create the first solar town in Puerto Rico. Some of the participating businesses include Gonzáles Hardware Store, Abreu Furniture Store, Jenny's Pharmacy, Limar Store, Lucy's Pizza, Osvaldo Hardware Store, Digital Point, Mueblicentro, and Hospice Services of Adjuntas, among others. The joint project, Adjuntas Solar Town, will be directed by Dr. Arturo Massol Deyá on behalf of Casa Pueblo, and the Honnold Foundation has designated Cinthia Arellano as the project's chief engineer. It took us a long time to get the project off the ground because we had to work out many details with internal and external actors before we could finally join forces for the common good. The wait was well worth it. This innovative, bottom-up community project is a continuation of the more than 150 solar energy micro-projects we've developed in Adjuntas since Hurricane María in 2017. Those micro-projects include the solarization of sixty homes, five markets, two hardware stores, two restaurants, a barbershop, an agricultural center, La Misericordia home for seniors, the fire station, and the emergency room. Additionally, we provided fifty-four solar refrigerators to rural homes, and distributed fourteen-thousand solar-powered portable lamps. Among the many small businesses and organizations that are collaborating with us are the Santa Ana Home for Girls, the Center for Children El Nuevo Hogar, the Vista al Río Restaurant, the Don Pepe Market in Vegas Abajo, the Cielo

Mar Market in Guilarte, the GoDestiny Bakery Shop in Lago, the Doña Lina Market in Tanamá, the La Olimpia Market in El Campo es Leña, and the Papún and El Gigante hardware stores.

The celebrations featured a screening of *Free Solo* in our Solar Cinema, followed by a Q&A with Alex Honnold, and a showing of our documentary *Nuestra insurrección energética* (*Our Energy Insurrection*, directed by Rhett Lee García Figueroa, 2019). The theater companies Y no había luz and Agua, Sol y Sereno participated in the cultural activities, as did the Orquesta Nacional Criolla Mapeyé, José Nogueras, and various folk singers, all in celebration of Earth Day. Finally, we presented this book, *Casa Pueblo cultiva esperanzas*, in its original Spanish version. The publication and Casa Pueblo's thirty-ninth anniversary coincide with a critical moment when we must seek answers to the great crisis in Puerto Rico, using alternative models to clear the way for a better tomorrow. Collective self-determination as it is affirmed in the streets is a democratic form of engagement. It pushes for change via alternative forms of self-sustainable development with popular support. A firm expression from our early years comes to mind: We have decided—no to the mines. As we bid farewell to 2019, the bright sun signaled an even brighter 2020.

CHAPTER 14

CASA PUEBLO IN TIMES OF COVID-19

The March of the Sun celebrates our freedom from fossil fuels and con-
solidates our model of community self-governance. April 21, 2019.

CASA PUEBLO'S FORTIETH ANNIVERSARY

We began to celebrate our 40th anniversary on January 11, 2020, the birthday of nineteenth-century Puerto Rican patriot and public intellectual Eugenio María de Hostos. On that day we paid homage to the memory of those no longer with us who have left their mark on the formation and the character of our community's self-governance, and who have contributed so much to Casa Pueblo's way of being, thinking, and approach to management. The event highlighted the philosophical principle of gratitude, which functions as an element of change, transformation, and education in life. At the end of that month, we inaugurated the solar power system at the Domingo Massol Rural School with a performance by the New York City Labor Chorus. By the end of February, we had finished the design for Adjuntas Solar Town, the project to solarize the urban center, and the installation of the solar panels finally began. Our 40th anniversary is special for many reasons, but especially because the government's Plan 2020 had set this year as the target date for the full operation of a network of seventeen open-pit mines to exploit for copper, gold, and silver in Adjuntas, Utuado, Lares, Jayuya, and the north of Ponce. Fifteen years of bitter struggle by many sectors of Puerto Rico's civil society stopped this destructive project and saved the island from an ecological and social catastrophe.

The anniversary provides an opportunity to reflect on how we have been able to keep community self-governance alive and politically independent for so long. Very briefly, five axioms define our work:

1. The concept of moving from protests, without discarding them, to propositions, created the basis for a self-sustaining community organization that is economically self-sufficient and ecologically self-sustainable. Some of the projects that have grown out of this concept include the purchase of a historic house in the center of town and its transformation into a visitor center and headquarters for Casa Pueblo,

Madre Isla Coffee, the Artisanal Shop, Casa Pueblo Radio, the Forest School, and the Community Music School.

2. The idea and practice of strategic community planning with a territorial focus toward the forests and the waters led, starting in 1996, to the designation of the People's Forest, The Olimpia Forest, the first biological corridor in Puerto Rico connecting five national forests, the Conservation Plan for Adjuntas and Adjacent Plans, and the Model Forest of Puerto Rico. This kind of strategic community planning led to the creation of the Fund for the Acquisition and Conservation of Lands in Puerto Rico to double Puerto Rico's protected lands from 5% to 10%.

3. The praxis from the bottom up has given rise to an innovative strategy of empowerment and social entrepreneurship. At its center is a robust, combative, resilient, and independent community that seeks social and political change for the common good.

4. The practice of communitarian social dialogue to reach agreements and form associations with external actors, who unite with and complement our efforts, capacities, and interests to reach a shared goal. This is the route we have taken for Adjuntas Solar Town, a project of self-sustainable and communitarian local development.

5. The equation *science + culture + community = change* functions as a holistic guide for a myriad of education projects that solidify the mission of Casa Pueblo.

THE COVID-19 PANDEMIC AND THE 2020 ELECTIONS

In March 2020, we received the first news of the COVID-19 pandemic. In the blink of an eye, projects, programs, and work plans came to a stop. The pandemic crisis upends the daily routines of our work, but the greatest loss is the connection with people and the brotherly and sisterly hugs with visitors and collaborators at the national and global levels. The conferences and interpretive tours at Casa Pueblo and in the forests for hundreds of students and so many others who came to visit weekly were all put on hold. It was surreal to see how suddenly and dramatically everything that we have been doing seven days a week for forty years suddenly came to a stop—indeed, they had to because of the epidemiological risks.

The COVID-19 humanitarian and public health crisis has wreaked havoc throughout the world, causing millions of people to become sick while hundreds of thousands continue to die. An unforeseen external agent has suddenly changed everything with grave social, economic, and political consequences. In the case of Puerto Rico, the government's response has been as inept as it was after Hurricane María in 2017 and the earthquakes of January 2020, both of which brought about enormous material and emotional damage. The lack of basic public services has become evident for everyone to see, especially in health and education. The quick succession of crises has kept a spotlight on the government's inept management of resources, its lack of transparency, and a culture of corruption that includes the outright theft of millions of dollars' worth of goods and resources. Understandably, public distrust of government officials is at an all-time high, as more and more people come to see this model of governance as primitive and obsolete. To be more precise, we are living under a model of governance that is neoliberal and colonial, embodied most recently in a federally imposed Financial Oversight and Management Board (FOMB, popularly known as la Junta) with dictatorial powers to rewrite the government's budget and impose austerity measures, among other powers. Under the Junta's de facto dictatorship, we have continued to hold elections where traditional and emerging political parties discuss how to administer the colony, searching in vain for ways to make substantive changes from the top down. This combination of factors puts us at a historical juncture, and the picture that emerges as we look to the future is nothing short of bleak. The coronavirus crisis alone negatively affects the life and the self-governance of our community. Many projects have come to a stop. We've had to observe physical distancing, which impedes the habitual greetings, the warm handshakes, the hugs, and the kisses. The levels of anxiety, frustration, anguish, fury, and uncertainty are all higher. Everything is about surviving and resisting in times that are complex, uncertain, and volatile. The situation requires that community self-governance redouble its efforts to overcome the circumstances. We must concentrate and maintain clarity of vision and the mission of self-governance to find a way out of this difficult situation. The response to the crisis generated by COVID-19 demands that we refocus, innovate, and promote creativity to address feelings of isolation and immobility.

PHYSICAL DISTANCING WITH SOCIAL RAPPROCHEMENT

The governing principle of coevolution in the social terrain plays an important role in ensuring that a community organization does not lose strength after it reaches its original goal or confronts a complex crisis. The former situation can produce the kind of triumphalism that immobilizes, while the latter can easily cause dispersion. For community self-governance to survive these traps, a double evolution must occur, an evolution in doing and being. The reciprocal interaction between both is what allows the active work of community organizing to continue. Based on this principle, for some years now we have been devising and implementing a process of harmonious transition in the relay of responsibilities and leadership. In this way, we have been expanding our work with an excellent group of volunteers comprising our board of directors, its president, and several consultants who are opening new paths forward to add those already open. This way, the old and the new embrace, ready to share in the historical task of responding to the crisis.

Our first security decision was to restrict access to the head-quarters of Casa Pueblo in the historic house we purchased in 1985. Only a nucleus of three volunteers—Tinti, Giorgie, and I—took on the task of maintaining minimal daily operations, including the upkeep of sensitive equipment. We limit physical visits to what is urgent and necessary. Communication takes place over the telephone and the internet, including virtual conferences. Everything else comes to a halt, including the people in charge. We observe. In the face of continued government calls for continued isolation, we respond with a formula of physical distancing with social rapprochement to get the wheels of our community moving again. This way, work done individually and at a distance begins to contribute toward a collective objective. Almost all the daily work of coordination is done at a distance and sometimes in person with the associate director. In the eye of the hurricane of COVID-19, answers and solutions flow to and from Casa Pueblo, passing through San Juan, Texas, San Francisco, and so many other places where we have loving collaborators and volunteers.

HEALTH ON THE AIRWAVES

Casa Pueblo Radio has stayed open and continues its work under rigorous health measures. The technical and administrative work continues with the same excellent personnel. New programs inform reliably on topics such as emotional and mental health, with sociologist Dr. Ruth Reyes; science and humanities, in a series produced by the Puerto Rican Endowment for the Humanities; earthquake updates with reliable information from the Seismic Web of Puerto Rico; current news, with Voices of the South; music and sports news, in a program called From A to Z; along with our regular programs like Songs of This Country Yours and Mine. Casa Pueblo Universitario, an initiative to bring university-level learning to the rural populations throughout Southern Puerto Rico, facilitates the production and distribution of a podcast on virology prepared by biology students at the University of Puerto Rico Ma-ya-güez. Casa Pueblo Universitario also coordinates research agendas and hands-on experiences in collaboration with the University of Puerto Rico, the University of Michigan, Notre Dame, Florida International University, the University of Central Florida, Yale, and the University of Idaho, among others. Through an agreement with the University of Puerto Rico in Río Piedras called PATRIA, we offer a series of virtual and radio workshops on resilience, leadership, public health, and education. Finally, the circumstances have led me to conduct a new program of interviews and analyses for Casa Pueblo Radio titled Casa Pueblo with the Community and Its People. Casa Pueblo Radio also retransmits live programs from other stations and television channels, including a series of video interviews titled "Women and Energy: Stories of Struggle in the Mountains" with reports by Michelle Estrada, photos by Ian Fohrman, and video by Rhett Lee Gracía. The work continues step by step, using digital platforms as bridges of communication to follow up on work plans, adjust programs, and coordinate tasks with our many collaborators. Patiently impatient, we continue our progress in the following areas:

RESTORATIONS AND ART PROJECTS

During these complicated times, we minimize participants' time physically interacting and maintain physical distancing when they must meet in person. Two months into the quarantine, some of the physical work begins again, starting with updates to the interior of Casa Puebla. Cheo and Jaime finish their work in about a month. After that, woodworking projects and an update of the electrical system begin for the Joaquín Parrilla Art Gallery, originally founded in 1984. In another room, Danny Torres (Adjuntas-born artist, Philadelphia resident, and longtime collaborator) restores a scale model of the planned mining operations that had been in storage, and he paints a mural celebrating the butterflies in our butterfly garden. Rebeca continues installing solar panels and refrigerators for domestic use, she also helps in the butterfly garden and completes other tasks.

THE CASA PUEBLO HISTORICAL DIGITAL ARCHIVE

The Casa Pueblo Historical Digital Archive grows out of an agreement with the Caribbean Diaspora Digital Humanities Center at the University of Puerto Rico Río Piedras, the School of General Studies, and the School of Humanities. This agreement will facilitate the exchange of knowledge between our organizations, provide opportunities for research and training for university students, and facilitate the development of curricular units that encourage reciprocal learning in a supportive environment. The initiative to digitally preserve documents, audiovisual materials, and artifacts will help us share Casa Puebla's history and the trajectory of our projects with the communities in Adjuntas and the world at large. We hope that the digital preservation of primary and secondary documents about our history will generate a space for reflection and serve as a model for similar projects based on community action. The Archive is working on two projects. First, Jesús Barriera is digitizing the historical documents that Tinti has been collecting over the years for use by historians and other interested researchers. For the second project, Elsa Castro and Inés Vélez, both teachers at the University Gardens School in San Juan, are preparing teaching units on community struggles for use in public schools throughout the island.

ONLINE ECONOMY

Our community social economy, which works with the social goal of maintaining the economic self-sufficiency of Casa Pueblo, came to a halt with the onset of the pandemic. We stopped earning income from the visits to the house, the forests, and the shop;

we stopped selling our coffee, Madre Isla. To address this challenge, in July we decided to start selling Madre Isla Coffee online through our website casapueblo.org. Roberto Riutort, originally from Adjuntas and now living in Oakland, made all the technical adjustments to our website for this to happen. People like Roberto who support our work and who drink high-quality coffee encouraged us to proceed with the initiative, and so again we begin the process of roasting, grinding, and packaging our Madre Isla Coffee. We understand that this new distribution format will permanently contribute to the social economy without replacing on-site visits to the coffee farm in the future. Fernando and Edwin restart their agro-ecological work at the coffee farm and expect a new harvest sometime between August and November. Regular and generous donations continue to arrive, and they help cover part of Casa Pueblo's payroll and other expenses.

AUDIO GUIDE FOR NATURE EDUCATION

A month into the quarantine, Cheo Pérez and Jaime González were back to the work of maintaining the Forest School, the Magic Mountain campground, and the Madre Isla Coffee Farm. By the last week of August, we were ready to reopen the Forest School for families to have an educational, healthy, and humanizing experience. This required three measures: creating an interpretive audio guide, developing infographics to detail the history of Casa Pueblo over the last 40 years, and setting up signs on the trails and in the open classrooms. Arturo Massol Deyá, in his role as associate director, oversees the audio guide with the help of others who work remotely. Roberto Riutort finishes reconfiguring the website for Casa Pueblo so that people can coordinate their visits and download the audio guide. The voice is that of journalist and performer Millie Gil who recorded the guide at her home in the San Juan metropolitan area. Coral Alicia is in charge of coordinating and supervising the visits to the forest. She also creates one of the artistic signs and the infographic on the history of Casa Pueblo. After a month of hard work, we can finally offer a tool to help families enjoy the forest at their own pace with the help of a digital map they can download to their cell phones or tablets, and each station is marked so that they can confirm that they are in the correct location. The first visits began the last week of August and we received positive feedback. Parallel to the audio guide, Arturo Massol Deyá produced an 11-minute video posted on our website that explains the role of forests in water security, and how the scientific method helps us to better understand nature. We soon follow the same protocol to reopen the Cerro Mágico camping area to allow families to enjoy its splendorous vistas of the entire island.

THE ENERGY INSURRECTION CONTINUES

We make the most of the downtime caused by the pandemic to adjust the design and placement of our modern system of photovoltaic batteries and to finalize our planned installation of solar panels in the urban core of the town of Adjuntas. Ideas travel back and forth in digital meetings between internal and external actors, strengthening our bonds in the process. Seven months into the pandemic, we resume the installation of solar panels and the energy insurrection we are calling Adjuntas Solar Town. Many of these solar panels were donated, some 250 used solar panels of 200 watts each, with an efficiency of around 90%. We devised three different ways of installing these panels so that almost anyone could do it by themselves. This way, those who are interested in participating in community self-governance can participate in the energy insurrection and help transform the energy ecosystem in Adjuntas and Puerto Rico. As she was in the immediate aftermath of Hurricane María, Tinti oversees selecting the participating families in a manner that is just and responsible.

A FEW LESSONS FROM THE BUTTERFLIES IN TIMES OF CRISIS

Tinti and I, in these times of physical distancing, have grown closer to the butterflies. The butterfly garden in the backyard of Casa Pueblo was inaugurated in 2001. Given the circumstances of the recent past, the garden was a bit abandoned, and so we set out to restore it to its previous splendor. The first thing we had to do was to reread books and documents and scour the internet to get up to date on the latest advances in lepidopterology, or the study of butterflies. We then updated the garden's management guide and the lab where the metamorphosis takes place. We planted host plants and nectar-producing flowers such as zinnias, cosmos, chamomile, calotropis, wild daisies, senna bicapsularis, and sunflowers. We also planted water hyacinths that bloomed quickly. After six months of work, the Monarch, the Phoebis, and the Julia butterflies danced the waltz of love to reproduce, and thus a project born nineteen years ago is reborn in times of COVID-19. The project began with one of the basic practices of community self-governance: self-education. First, we purchased books and began to learn about the topic. Then we visited butterfly gardens and farms in different countries, including the one in the Iguazú National Park in Argentina, a feast for the eyes. We began to write our first user's guide on how to construct and manage a butterfly garden. Next, we built a scale model as a first step in going from theory to practice. The best part was visiting different neighborhoods to learn from people in the countryside about which plants attract butterflies. We planted them, and before long, we were looking for butterfly eggs and larvae. The design and construction of the full-scale garden were overseen by Francisco Pérez, a Puerto Rican artist I met in 1984 in San Francisco during an anti-mining campaign tour of eight states in the United States. Seventeen years later, he visited us during his sabbatical. On April 22, 2001, we celebrated the completion of his project and the twenty-first anniversary of Casa Pueblo. José Ballester Panelli, son of Edna and Jossie (who had contributed to the anti-mining campaign), designed a poster for the occasion. Carmen Lidia Acosta, a theater teacher at the Adjuntas High School, staged a play with her students, and there was music and a wonderful audience smitten by the project.

Butterflies teach us many lessons, and they are such beautiful, elegant, and moving creatures that they also bring us happiness. Even their name is enchanting and makes us think of something mythical, magical, and special. In the ancient Mexican cultures, butterflies symbolized the souls of dead warriors returning to their communities as butterflies. For me, they bring back vivid memories of my son Ariel, one of the many people who helped turn the idea of a butterfly garden into a reality. In other ancient cultures, butterflies represent the need for change and liberty, evident in the marvelous process that is their metamorphosis. They constantly transform, starting as an egg, which becomes a larva, and then a chrysalis. Finally, the butterfly breaks the walls that held it captive, emerging to open its wings and ready to begin its flight of liberty. A recent study of fossils places the origin of Lepidoptera (the order of insects to which butterflies belong) to two hundred million years ago when dinosaurs still roamed our planet. At one point those enormous and powerful creatures became extinct, while the fragile and beautiful butterflies lived on to sweeten the soul of humanity. The brilliant lessons from our pollinating friends in times of crisis help us to not feel weak, isolated, or impotent in the face of a public health crisis whose roots are political, economic, and ultimately colonial.

SOME REFLECTIONS AND PROVISIONAL CONCLUSIONS

Casa Pueblo is a model of community self-governance that, through many struggles and many economic, ecological, energetic, educational, and cultural sustainability projects, has been generating changes from the local to the national level. Because of the nature of our work, we continuously confront the colonial structures that perpetuate inequality, dependency, and a sense of helplessness in the face of challenges. Against the odds, we have been able to win battle after battle over the past forty years. After a failed first public event in 1980, only three of us, Tinti Deyá, Noemilda Vélez, and I, stayed in the organization while the rest blamed Puerto Rico's entrenched colonial mindset to avoid personal responsibility. Truly, the three of us felt alone, isolated, and desperate. We felt impotent and did not know how to face the challenge. But just like the Julián Chiví, the Black-whiskered vireo, we took flight using innovative and alternative strategies to earn back the love of the people so that they could defend what was rightfully theirs. Out of necessity, we developed a capacity to face adversity with both imagination and combativeness. The strategy paid off fifteen years later, with the end to all mining in 1995. That was just the beginning. Casa Pueblo in Adjuntas now faces the COVID-19 pandemic and again transforms a crisis into an opportunity. We are creatively evolving and strengthening the institution and embracing one another at a distance while keeping socially connected. Still hopeful, we continue to build utopias and collective dreams.

Today's great challenge is imagining that another country is possible, that another world is possible. And if the imagining is difficult, it is even harder to find ways to turn that vision into a reality. And yet, despite the difficulties, we see countless examples of resistance, struggle, and alternative projects in every corner of Planet Earth. "Fortunately," as Arizaldo Carvajal Burbano writes, "there are towns and localities that are trying out alternative development models and new ways of being in society. In a context of despair and authoritarian gestures, of exclusion, new bets and processes are emerging that allow us to dream once again, to help us believe that another world is possible."[1] This book has articulated and theorized about the experiences and initiatives of one such example, Casa Pueblo, over forty years. Our path has been marked by successes and failures but we have never wavered in our commitment to community self-governance and self-determination. This is how we evolved beyond protesting (without discarding it as a tactic), to proposing and carrying out projects promoting economic self-sufficiency, ecological diversity, solar energy, and cultural education.

Our struggles align with many of the fundamental elements that define Puerto Rico's territory, language, culture, economy, and social community, all elements that work together to defend the common good. The model advances and grows with a new paradigm of community-based development that is locally rooted, nationally resonant, and global in scope. With patience and determination, we have been building from the bottom up. We aim to break the chains of economic, ideological, and political dependence imposed by the colonial-metropolitan model. Like a master craftsperson with a chisel, Casa Pueblo carves a path to a new reality and an alternative model for the country. Looking into the future with a powerful lens, we could prophesize a young star appearing on the horizon whose green light reveals the new utopia.

I invite you to join us!

Notes

INTRODUCTION

1. Gregory Fernando Pappas, "Horizontal Models of 'Conviviality' or Radical Democracy in the Americas: Zapatistas (Chiapas, Mexico), Boggs Center (Detroit, USA), Casa Pueblo (Adjuntas, Puerto Rico)" in Mecila working paper series (forthcoming).
2. Alexis Massol González, Email, January 6, 2021.

CHAPTER 5

1. Clarence Beardsley, "ELA compraría terrenos de minas," *El Mundo* (San Juan, PR), Aug. 26, 1986.

CHAPTER 6

1. *El Vocero*, June 23, 1993, p. 9.
2. Carolay Morales, "El Amazonas Tiene Más 6 Mil Solicitudes Para Explotación Minera En Zonas Protegidas: WWF," RCN Radio, June 26, 2016, https://www.rcnradio.com/medio-ambiente/el-amazonas-tiene-mas-6-mil-solicitudes-para-explotacion-minera-en-zonas-protegidas-wwf.
3. Ernesto J. Navarro. "Minería a Gran Escala Atenta Contra El Nevado Pastoruri De Perú." RT en Español, September 2, 2016. https://actualidad.rt.com/actualidad/217729-agotan-nieves-pastoruri-peru.

4. "Empresa Minerales de Occidente hace desaparecer comunidad entera en Copán," Observatorio de Conflictos Mineros de América Latina, August 22, 2016, https://www.ocmal.org/empresa-minerales-de-occidente-hace-desa-parecer-comunidad-enteras-en-copan/.

5. "Director del Banco Mundial justifica el asesinato de Berta Cáceres . . . ," accessed October 25, 2021, https://noalamina.org/latinoamerica/honduras/item/15608-director-del-banco-mundial-justifica-el-asesinato-de-berta-ca-ceres.

CHAPTER 7

1. Gaston Bachelard. *The Poetics of Space*. New York: Penguin Classics, 2014.

2. Braulio Zerecero Cisneros (2014). "El concepto de topofilia en geografía: una forma novedosa de explicar la apropiación de los espacios desde el sujeto." En *Tintas de Geografía*. México. http://antridigeo.blogspot.mx/2014/11/el-con-ceptode-topofilia-en-geografia.html. Accessed 12/01/2018.

3. Francisco Garrido Peña. "Topofília, paisatge i sostenibilitat del territori." *Enrahonar: An International Journal of Theoretical and Practical Reason* 53 (2014): 63-75.

4. Gaston Bachelard. T*The Poetics of Space*. New York: Penguin Classics, 2014.

CHAPTER 9

1. José Martí, *Versos sencillos* (1891), trans. Manuel A. Tellechea. Allpoetry.com, https://allpoetry.com/I-Have-a-White-Rose-to-Tend-(Verse-XXXIX) (accessed October 23, 2021).

CHAPTER 11

1. "Commonwealth of Puerto Rico, Petitioner vs. Luis M. Sánchez Valle, et al." 136 S.Ct. 1863 (2016), https://www.scotusblog.com/wp-content/uploads/2015/12/US-amicus-brief-in-Valle-15-108.pdf, Accessed October 8, 2021.

2. Naomi Klein, *The Battle for Paradise: Puerto Rico Takes on the Disaster Capitalists*. Chicago: Haymarket Books, 2018, p. 26.

3. José de Diego, *Cantos de rebeldía*. Barcelona: Casa Editorial Maucci, 1917, p. 68.

4. Kahlil Gibran, in *The Wisdom of the Great*, ed. Sam Madji. Bloomington, IN: iUniverse, 2012, p. 511.

CHAPTER 12

1. Mercedes Alcañiz Moscardó. "El desarrollo local en el contexto de la globalización." *Convergencia* [online] 15, n. 47 (2008): 310.
2. Subcomandante Marcos, *¡Ya basta! Ten years of the Zapatista Uprising. Writings of Subcomandante Insurgente Marcos*. Ed. Ziga Vodovnik. Oakland, CA: AK Press, 2004, p. 271.
3. Ana Lúcia Souza de Freitas, *Pedagogia do Concientização: Um Legado de Paulo Freire a Formação de Professores,* third edition. Porto Alegre: EDIPUCRS, 2004, p. 156.
4. Alcañiz Moscardó, "El desarrollo local," p. 285.
5. Alcañiz Moscardó, "El desarrollo local," p. 285.
6. José Arocena, *El desarrollo local como desafío contemporáneo*, second edition. Montevideo: Universidad Católica, 2002, p 7.
7. Augusto Boal, *Teatro del oprimido 1*, trans. Graciela Schmilchuk. Mexico City: Nueva Imagen, 1980, p. 120.

CHAPTER 13

1. Sergio Boisier. "Desarrollo (local): ¿de qué estamos hablando?" (1999), http://municipios.unq.edu.ar/modules/mislibros/archivos/29-DesLo.pdf. Accessed October 8, 2021.

CHAPTER 14

1. Arizaldo Carvajal Burbano, ¿Modelos alternativos de desarrollo o modelos alternativos al desarrollo? *Prospectiva: Revista de Trabajo Social e Intervención Social*, no. 14 (2009), DOI: https://doi.org/10.25100/prts.v0i14.1095, Accessed October 8, 2021.

Bibliography

Alcañiz, Moscardó, Mercedes. "El desarrollo local en el contexto de la globalización." *Convergencia* [online] 15, n. 47 (2008): 285-315.

Arocena, José. "Globalización, integración y desarrollo local." In *Transformaciones globales, instituciones y políticas de desarrollo local.* Eds. Antonio Vázquez Barquero and Oscar Madoery. Rosario, Argentina: Homo Sapiens Ediciones, 2001.

Asencio Yace, Jehyra Marie. *Las aguas, los bosques y sus gentes. Una respuesta comunitaria a la crisis de desarrollo actual en el proyecto de autogestión Casa Pueblo del municipio de Adjuntas, Puerto Rico.* Master's Thesis, University of Brasilia, Brazil, 2013.

Azam, Geneviève (2009). "Economía solidaria y reterritorialización de la economía." *Pampa* [Toulouse: Université Toulouse II] 1, no. 5, (2009): 69-77.

Bachelard, Gaston. *The Poetics of Space.* New York: Penguin Classics, 2014.

Boisier, Sergio. "El territorio en la contemporaneidad (la recuperación de las políticas territoriales)." *Líder: Revista Labor Interdisciplinaria de Desarrollo Regional* [Universidad de Los Lagos, Chile] n. 18 (2011): 9-24.

Capel, Horacio. "Las ciencias sociales y el estudio del territorios." *Biblio 3W: Revista Bibliográfica de Geografía y Ciencias Sociales* [University of Barcelona] 21, n. 1,149 (2016): 1-38.

Carson, Rachel L. *Silent Spring.* Boston: Houghton Mifflin, 1962.

Colón Rivera, J., Córdova Iturregui, F., and Córdova Iturregui, J. *El proyecto de explotación minera en Puerto Rico (1962-1968): Nacimiento de la conciencia ambiental moderna.* San Juan, Puerto Rico: Ediciones Huracán, 2014.

Deyá Díaz, Tinti. "Ante los ultrajes a la vida, la felicidad y la libertad del pueblo puertorriqueño." Presentation given in representation of the Arts and Culture Workshop of Adjuntas, before the United Nations Special Committee on Decolonization, 1983.

Durston, John. ¿Qué es el capital social comunitario? Santiago: United Nations/ CEPAL, 2000.

Energy Globe Award. https://www.energyglobe.info/, 2015.

Fernandes, Bernardo Mançano. "Movimientos socioterritoriales y movimientos socioespaciales. Contribución teórica para una lectura geográfica de los movimientos sociales." Revista NERA [University of São Paulo] n. 6, vol. 8 (2005): 24-34.

Figueres, Albert. Emprendedores sociales: todos podemos cambiar el mundo. Barcelona: Plataforma Editorial, 2011.

Garrido Peña, Francisco. "Topofilia: paisaje y sostenibilidad del territorio." Enrahonar: An International Journal of Theoretical and Practical Reason, n. 53 (2014): 63-75.

Gasca Zamora, José. "Gobernanza y gestión comunitaria de recursos naturales en la Sierra Norte de Oaxaca." Región y sociedad, vol. 26, n. 60 (2014): 89-120.

Goldman Environmental Prize, 2002. Accessed October 2, 2021, https://www. goldmanprize.org/recipient/alexis-massol-gonzalez/

Hostos, Eugenio María de. Puerto Rico, Madre Isla (Primera Parte) 1898. [Volume V, number II of the Complete Works.] San Juan: University of Puerto Rico; Institute of Hostos Studies, 2001.

Junta de Planificación de Puerto Rico. Plan de Conservación para Adjuntas y Municipios Adyacentes, 2004. Accessed October 2, 2021, http://jp.pr.gov/Portals/0/Planes%20Sectoriales/Planes/PLAN%20CONSERV%20AREAS%20 SENSIT%20(PCAS)%20ADJUNTAS%20red2.pdf?ver=2017-05-10-152640-450

Ley Bosque Modelo de Puerto Rico, 2015. Accessed October 2, 2021, http:// drna.pr.gov/wp-content/uploads/2015/05/P.-de-la-C.-1635-Proyecto-de-ley-Bosque-Modelo.pdf

Magnaghi, Alberto. The Urban Village: A Charter for Democracy and Local Self-Sustainable Development. Trans. David Kerr. Plymouth, UK: Zed Books, 2005.

Martínez Valle, Luciano. "Apuntes para pensar el territorio desde una dimensión social." Ciencias Sociais Unisinos [São Leopoldo, Brasil], vol. 48, n. 1 (2012): 12-18.

Maritza, Montero. Introducción a la psicología comunitaria. Diseño, conceptos y procesos. Buenos Aires: Editorial Paidós, 2004.

Martín-Baró, Ignacio. "Hacia una psicología de la liberación." Psicología Sin Fronteras: Revista Electrónica de Intervención Psicosocial y Psicología Comunitaria

[Universidad Centroamericana José Simeón Cañas, El Salvador], vol. 1, n. 2 (2006): 7-14.

Massol Deyá, Arturo, and Díaz de Osborne, E. *Ciencia y ecología: Vieques en crisis ambiental.* Adjuntas: Publicaciones Casa Pueblo, third edition, 2002. Accessed October 2, 2021, http://vieques.uprm.edu/documents/libro.pdf

Massol González, Alexis. *De la deformación a la destrucción.* Chicago: Editorial El Coquí, 1983.

---. *Plan 2020 y la explotación minera.* Adjuntas: Editorial Casa Pueblo, 1985.

Massol González, Alexis; Andromache Johnnidis, A.; and Massol Deyá, A. (2008). "The Evolution of Casa Pueblo, Puerto Rico. From Mining Opposition to Community Revolution." London: International Institute for Environment and Development [Working Paper Series].

Massol González, Alexis, González, E.; Massol Deyá, A.; Deyá Díaz, T.; and Geoghegan, T. (2006). *Bosque del Pueblo, Puerto Rico: How a fight to stop a mine ended up changing forest policy from the bottom up.* London: International Institute for Environment and Development [Case Study Series]. Accessed October 2, 2021, https://pubs.iied.org/13503IIED/

Merino, Amparo, et. al. *Guía del emprendedor social. Inspiraciones para la creación de empresas al servicio de la sociedad.* Madrid: Universidad Pontificia ICAI, 2013.

Olivera, Marcus Eduardo de. "Por una economía comunitaria y social: la vida es el valor central." *Contribuciones a la Economía,* v. 10 (2010): 16-17.

Quiroga, Hiram; Santiago, Quevedo; and Chirigoba, Eduardo. *Hacia el cambio mediante la autogestión.* Quito: CONADE, 1995.

Ruggeri, Andrés. *Autogestión y economía solidaria.* Bilbao: REAS Euskadi, 2012.

Ruiz Sierra, A., Aponte, L., et.al., eds. *Casa Pueblo de Puerto Rico. El co-manejo del Bosque del Pueblo y la gobernanza de los recursos naturales comunes.* San Juan: Universidad de Puerto Rico, Serie Ocasional de Estudios de Casos Multimedios, 2010.

Salinas Ramos, Francisco, and Osorio Bayter, Lourdes. "Emprendimiento y economía social, oportunidades y efectos en una sociedad en transformación." *CIRIEC-España: Revista de Economía Pública, Social, y Cooperativa,* no. 75 (2012): 129-151.

Saballos Vélasquez, José Luis. *La universidad y la efectividad del desarrollo comunitario.* Doctoral thesis. University of the Basque Country, 2016. Accessed October 3, 2021, https://dialnet.unirioja.es/servlet/tesis?codigo=112045

Sébastien, Viaud. *Résistants pour la Terre. Les lauréates et lauréats du Prix Goldman, le "Nobel de l'environment".* Vannes [France]: Viatao-Liberta, 2009.

Santos, Milton. *De la totalidad al lugar.* Trad. María Laura Silveira. Barcelona: Oikos-Tau, 1996.

Sousa, Angela. *Protesta, propuesta y evolución: un análisis de las estrategias educativas de Casa Pueblo para la participación social contra la explotación minera en Puerto Rico, 1980-1996.* Master's Thesis. FLACSO Argentina, 2018.

Toro Muñoz, Zulma Zorayda. "Territorio lugar: Espacio de resistencia y lucha de los movimientos sociales." *Pacarina del sur: Revista de pensamiento crítico latinoamericano*, vol. 1, no. 11, 2012. Accessed October 2, 2021, http://pacarinadelsur.com/home/abordajes-y-contiendas/421-territorio-lugar-espacio-de-resistencia-y-lucha-de-los-movimientos-sociales

Touraine, Alain. "Los movimientos sociales." *Revista Colombiana de Sociología*, no. 27, (2006): 255-278.

Tuan, Yi-Fu. *Topophilia: A Study of Environmental Perception, Attitudes, and Values.* New York: Columbia University Press, 1974.

Yory, Carlos Mario. "El concepto de topofilia entendido como teoría del lugar." Accessed October 2, 2021, http://academico2.tripod.com/topofilia.pdf

Les Vagabonds de l'énergie. *Porto Rico: Du local au global á Casa Pueblo, 2017.* Accessed October 8 2021, https://www.youtube.com/watch?v=8G4qLEDRdoY&feature=emb_logo

Zaragoza Ramírez, Miguel Ángel. *Movimientos sociales en México. Apuntes teóricos y estudios de casos.* Mexico City: Universidad Metropolitana, 2016.

Zayas Oliveras, Herminia. *Análisis de veinte años en la lucha ambiental de Puerto Rico de 1980 a 2000.* Master's Thesis in Environmental Science, Universidad Interamericana de Puerto Rico, San Germán campus, 2006. Accessed October 2, 2021, http://ponce.inter.edu/cai/Tesis_Graduado/hzayas/index.pdf

Zerecero Cisneros, Braulio. "El concepto de topofilia en geografía: Una forma novedosa de explicar la apropiación de los espacios desde el sujeto," 2014. Accessed October 2, 2021, http://antridigeo.blogspot.com/2014/11/el-concepto-de-topofilia-en-geografia.html

CPSIA information can be obtained
at www.ICGtesting.com
Printed in the USA
BVHW061929260322
632430BV00007B/73